Passive Income: How to Use Cry

Create Automatic Monthly Income

By Stephen Satoshi

The following eBook is reproduced below with the goal of providing information that is as accurate and reliable as possible. Regardless, purchasing this eBook can be seen as consent to the fact that both the publisher and the author of this book are in no way experts on the topics discussed within and that any recommendations or suggestions that are made herein are for entertainment purposes only. Professionals should be consulted as needed prior to undertaking any of the action endorsed herein.

This declaration is deemed fair and valid by both the American Bar Association and the Committee of Publishers Association and is legally binding throughout the United States.

Furthermore, the transmission, duplication or reproduction of any of the following work including specific information will be considered an illegal act irrespective of if it is done electronically or in print. This extends to creating a secondary or tertiary copy of the work or a recorded copy and is only allowed with express written consent from the Publisher. All additional right reserved.

The information in the following pages is broadly considered to be a truthful and accurate account of facts and as such any inattention, use or misuse of the information in question by the reader will render any resulting actions solely under their purview. There are no scenarios in which the publisher or the original author of this work can be in any fashion deemed liable for any hardship or damages that may befall them after undertaking information described herein.

Additionally, the information in the following pages is intended only for informational purposes and should thus be thought of as universal. As befitting its nature, it is presented without assurance regarding its prolonged validity or interim quality. Trademarks that are mentioned are done without written consent and can in no way be considered an endorsement from the trademark holder.

Financial Disclaimer:

I am not a financial advisor, this is not financial advice. This is not an investment guide nor investment advice. I am not recommending you buy any of the coins listed here. Any form of investment or trading is liable to lose you money.

There is no single "best" investment to be made, in cryptocurrencies or otherwise. Anyone telling you so is deceiving you.

I am not affiliated with any coin or cryptocurrency mentioned in this book.

There is no "surefire coin" - one again, anyone telling you so is deceiving you.

With many coins, especially the smaller ones, the market is liable to the spread of misinformation.

Never invest more than you are willing to lose. Cryptocurrency is not a get rich quick scheme.

Income Disclaimer:

The book may refer to business opportunities or other money-making opportunities. If any such content exists in this book, the following disclaimers apply.

You recognize and agree that we have made no implications, warranties, promises, suggestions, projections, representations or guarantees whatsoever to you about future prospects or earnings, or that you will earn any money, with respect to your purchase of books by Stephen Satoshi, and that we have not authorized any such projection, promise, or representation by others.

Any earnings or income statements, or any earnings or income examples, are only estimates of what we think you could earn. There is no assurance you will do as well as stated in any examples. If you rely upon any figures provided, you must accept the entire risk of not doing as well as the information provided. This applies whether the earnings or income examples are monetary in nature or pertain to advertising credits which may be earned (whether such credits are convertible to cash or not).

There is no assurance that any prior successes or past results as to earnings or income (whether monetary or advertising credits, whether convertible to cash or not) will apply, nor can any prior successes be used, as an indication of your future success or results from any of the information, content, or strategies. Any and all claims or representations as to income or earnings (whether monetary or advertising credits, whether convertible to cash or not) are not to be considered as "average earnings".

The Economy. The economy, both where you do business, and on a national and even worldwide scale, creates additional uncertainty and economic risk. An economic recession or depression might negatively affect the results produced by Stephen Satoshi.

Your Success Or Lack Of It. Your success in using the information or strategies provided by Stephen Satoshi depends on a variety of factors. We have no way of knowing how well you will do, as we do not know you, your background, your work ethic, your dedication, your motivation, your desire, or your business skills or practices. Therefore, we do not guarantee or imply that you will get rich, that you will do as well, or that you will have any earnings (whether monetary or advertising credits, whether convertible to cash or not), at all.

Contents

Contents 5

Cryptocurrency: Insider Secrets 2 - 10 Exciting Crypto Projects With Potential for Explosive Growth in 2018 7

Free Bonus! ....**Error! Bookmark not defined.**

Special Offer for Audible Customers ....**Error! Bookmark not defined.**

Introduction - The Current State of the Cryptocurrency Market 8

Factors to Consider Before Investing 10

How to Buy Bitcoin, Ethereum & Litecoin in Under 15 Minutes 13

How to buy Altcoins 14

Transferring your newly purchased Bitcoin to your exchange of choice. 16

Storing Your Coins - How to set up MyEtherWallet 17

10 High Potential Coins Under $1 19

How to Buy Coins on Coinbase With Zero Transaction Fees 51

A Brand New Way to Buy Cryptocurrency Which Could Have Huge Market Ramifications 53

Things You Need to Be Aware of With Certain Cryptocurrency Channels on YouTube 54

Conclusion 56

Cryptocurrency: Mining for Beginners - How You Can Make Up To $18,500 a Year Mining Coins From Home 57

Introduction 58

Basic Overview of Mining Cryptocurrencies 59

Buying GPUs 63

Proof of Work vs. Proof of Stake 64

Why I Don't Recommend You Mine Bitcoin 66

Ethereum's Switch from Proof of Work to Proof of Stake Protocols 72

Mining Versus Buying Cryptocurrencies 75

How to Setup your Own Mining Rig 80

What is Cloud Mining? 88

List of Noted   Mining Scams to Avoid 91

An Introduction to Mobile Mining 94

How to Make Money Staking Coins 98

Most Profitable Proof of Stake Cryptocurrencies 99

Mining based stocks - An often overlooked opportunity 102

Another Cryptocurrency Lending Scheme to Be Wary Of 104

Conclusion 105

Cryptocurrency: FAQ - Answering 53 of Your Burning Questions about Bitcoin, Investing, Scams, ICOs and Trading 106

Introduction.. 107

Bitcoin 108

Cryptocurrency Investing 116

ICOs.. 124

Altcoins... 128

Miscellaneous Questions 143

Conclusion 152

Other Books by Stephen Satoshi...**Error! Bookmark not defined.**

Cryptocurrency: Insider Secrets 2 - 10 Exciting Crypto Projects With Potential for Explosive Growth in 2018

By Stephen Satoshi

Introduction - The Current State of the Cryptocurrency Market

Well, there's never a dull day in the crypto market and the start to 2018 has been no exception. We've seen record highs hit in December and January for a number of coins. Bitcoin reached $19,800, Ethereum topped $1,000 for the first time and Ripple soared to above $3. Since then the news has been more muted, and the market has been moving sideways and downwards for the past couple of months. Now before you think it's all doom and gloom, let's take a few minutes to examine why this movement isn't the worst thing in the world, and what we can expect from the crypto market in the rest of the years.

First of all, we must examine what has been causing the recent price slides. There are a number of reasons for this. The first blow came when it was revealed that a number of credit cards companies were banning users from making cryptocurrency purchases on their cards. This is a step forward as it is in line with other financial instruments. For example, no licensed stock trading website will allow credit card deposits, so crypto applying the same rules is a move in a right direction.

Secondly, we had the federal investigations into Tether, the cryptocurrency that is pegged to the US dollar. In late January, the US Commodity Futures Trading Commision (CTFC) began an investigation into Bitfinex and Tether. Tether claimed that all of its coins were backed by actual US dollars held in reserve, but failed to prove this was the case. Tether nevertheless denied accusations. Bitfinex was dragged into the battle because both companies share the same CEO. This caused the price of crypto to drop as some commentators believed Tethers were being printed to artificially inflate Bitcoin prices. If this is indeed the case, then we as investors should be willing to accept short term losses for a more stable long term market.

The third and final piece of bad news came out of Japan. The Japanese Financial Services Agency fined 7 different cryptocurrency exchanges for not following regulatory rules. The same agency then ordered two other agencies to suspend business altogether. This move came after Tokyo-based firm Coincheck had $530 million worth of cryptocurrency stolen. This news caused the market to drop by 5.3% in a single day. Once again, we should encourage a crackdown on poorly run exchanges if it means long term market stability.

Now, let's get on to the good news. After a senate hearing on cryptocurrency, CFTC chairman Chris Giancarlo made a number of bullish statements on cryptocurrency and blockchain technology. Giancarlo's most poignant line was "We owe it to this new generation to respect their enthusiasm for virtual currencies, with a thoughtful and balanced response, and not a dismissive one." A stance like this from the head of one of the most powerful financial regulatory committees in the US is only going to be a positive - both for consumer and institutional investors. Giancarlo then went onto discussing the benefits of blockchain technology and even discussed the term "HODL" in his speech. Financial regulators will support cryptocurrencies if it means people can make money with them through non-nefarious means. If they have to step in to prevent theft, hacking and use for criminal activity, then so be it.

Speaking on institutional adoption, March brought news of the Coinbase Index Fund. I discuss this later on in this book and what it could mean for crypto going forward, but needless to say, any kind of large scale institutional adoption is only going to be a good thing for cryptocurrency as a whole.

So without further ado, let's move forward and examine some of the best cryptocurrency projects in 2018, and see exactly how you can get involved.

Thanks,

Stephen

Factors to Consider Before Investing

While larger cryptocurrencies like Bitcoin, Ethereum and Litecoin have long track records and multiple real world functions, some of the coins mentioned in this book do not - hence their lower price.

There are a number of different variables to investigate before you undertake any investment, and cryptocurrency has its own set.

Proof of Concept (PoC)

In other words, does the technology have a working model, or is it still in a theoretical stage. Obviously more mature coins will have a higher value, with the more theoretical coins being a bigger risk. As the different coins here are in different stages of their life cycle, that is up for you to decide.

The development team

Who are the developers and what is their track record? Particularly within the cryptocurrency and blockchain space. Another thing to consider is their record within the particular industry they are targeting.

The whitepaper

A good whitepaper discusses the technical aspects of the coin, in a way that the average investor can understand. Many low quality crypto projects take shortcuts in their whitepaper and tend to fill it with hypey language rather than actual technological information. If a whitepaper doesn't discuss exactly how the project works, then that is a huge red flag.

The utility of the token

Ideas are great, but if the coin token itself doesn't have usage, then the true potential of the project must be questioned. This is especially true in the case of certain coins where the theory and market potential checks out, but the question of "why can we just use Bitcoin/Litecoin to do the same thing" is often raised.

The roadmap

Roadmaps are important for short-term gains because they set out development targets for the coin. If these goals are reached and the products/platforms move from alpha to beta to a fully launched product, then that only means positive things for the coin and its value. If a team consistently meets targets on or before a deadline, then we can look at that as a positive sign.

Which exchanges the coin is listed on

Many of these coins are still only available on smaller exchanges. Once the coin is listed on larger exchanges (for example Binance), the coin has greater visibility and this leads to a rise in value.

Mining Algorithms - Proof of Work vs. Proof of Stake vs. Others

You'll notice later on when discussing individual coins that I sometimes talk about which mining algorithms are used. The two most popular are Proof of Work (PoW), used by Bitcoin and Proof of Stake (PoS), used by coins like Neo, Stellar Lumens, Ark and a number of Ethereum based tokens. Ethereum plans to move to Proof of Stake in 2018.

In my previous book *Bitcoin: Beginners Bible* I discussed why I don't recommend mining as an effective method for obtaining cryptocurrency, for the regular user. That still holds true for the majority of the coins listed in this book, but it's important to understand why the difference in mining algorithm matters.

Why do we need mining?

We need mining to ensure a transaction (or block) is correctly validated, in other words, we need to ensure the same transaction doesn't occur twice - known as the double spending problem. As a reward for validating this transaction, miners are rewarded with a tiny percentage of it (known as the network fee).

To put it bluntly, Proof of Work takes a lot more energy than Proof of Stake. A 2015 study showed that one Bitcoin transaction takes the equivalent daily energy of 1.57 US homes. Proof of Stake is also a fairer, more energy efficient system, which is a huge advantage for community based coins.

Other systems include Delegated Proof of Stake (DPoS), which is a more community based initiative. DPoS is where stakeholders vote for delegates to make decisions for them, allowing both parties to profit from those decisions.

How to Buy Bitcoin, Ethereum & Litecoin in Under 15 Minutes

Gone are the days when buying Bitcoin was a time consuming and somewhat uncomfortable endeavor. Nowadays buying Bitcoin is a similar process to exchanging currency when you go on vacation.

There are two ways to buy Bitcoin, the first is to use fiat currency (USD, Euros, GBP etc.) to purchase cryptocurrency via an exchange. These exchanges function the same way as regular foreign currency exchanges do. The prices fluctuate on a daily basis, and like regular currency exchange markets - they are open 24/7. These exchanges make their money from charging a small fee for each transaction.

Some charge both buyers and sellers, some only charge a fee for buying. For security reasons, most of these exchanges will require you to verify your ID before allowing you to purchase cryptocurrency.

It is also important to note the type of payments each exchange supports. Some allow for debit/credit card payments whereas other only accept PayPal or bank wire transfers. Below are the three biggest and reputable currency exchanges for purchasing Bitcoin, Ethereum and other altcoins with fiat currency like US dollars, Euros or British Pounds.

Coinbase

Currently largest currency exchange in the world, Coinbase allows users to buy, sell and store cryptocurrency. Coinbase is undoubtedly the most beginner friendly exchange for anyone looking to get involved in the cryptocurrency market. They currently allow trading of Bitcoin, as well as, Ethereum and LiteCoin using fiat currency as a base. As of January 1st 2018, you can now buy Bitcoin Cash on Coinbase as well. Known for their stellar security procedures and insurance policies regarding stored currency. The exchange also has a fully functioning iPhone and Android app for buying and selling on the go, very useful if you are looking to trade.

Once you are signed up and complete the identity verification procedures you can buy Bitcoin with your credit or debit card instantly.

Coinbase also recently launched the Coinbase Vault, which is a secure way of storing your cryptocurrency while still having it accessible to trade. The vault uses double email address + phone verification in order to access your funds. If you're planning on holding long-term, I still recommend offline storage - but as an intermediary option, the Vault is a step in the right direction.

If you sign up for Coinbase using this link, you will receive $10 worth of free Bitcoin after your first purchase of more than $100 worth of cryptocurrency.

http://bit.ly/10dollarbtc

Note, if you're going to be trading Bitcoin, I recommend doing so on Coinbase's partner platform GDax, which has lower fees.

How to buy Altcoins

The vat majority of cryptocurrency projects cannot be bought directly for fiat currency. They require you to buy Bitcoin or Ethereum first and then exchanging that into these altcoins.

Binance

My personal favorite altcoin exchange, and the one with the most liquidity on a number of coins. Binance has over 100 cryptocurrencies available, and nearly all of them now have both BTC and ETH trade pairings.

Their support is top notch, and probably the best of any exchange. You'll have to transfer the coins to a wallet if you want to securely store them long-term, but for buying and trading altcoins - you can't go wrong with Binance.

Poloniex

With more than 100 different cryptocurrencies available and data analysis for advanced traders, Poloniex is the most comprehensive exchange on the market. Low trading fees are another plus, this is a great place to trade your Bitcoin into other cryptocurrencies. If you have never purchased Bitcoin before, you will no be able to do so as Poloniex does not allow fiat currency deposits. Therefore, you will have to make your initial Bitcoin purchases on Coinbase or Kraken.

Other sites I have personally used to purchase cryptocurrency include Liqui and Cryptopia. Please do your due diligence when selecting which exchange to buy and store coins on, and ensure you are always typing the correct web address to avoid phishing sites.

Transferring your newly purchased Bitcoin to your exchange of choice.

Once you have bought your Bitcoin from Coinbase/Kraken, you'll need to then transfer it over to Binance, Bittrex or whichever exchange your coin of choice is listed on. To do this, simply go to the exchange you need to transfer the coins to (e.g. Bittrex) and click on "deposit", choose BTC (remember to double check you've clicked the correct coin). This will generate an address that looks like this 1F1tAaz5x1HUXrCNLbtMDqcw6o5GNn4xqX

From there, go to your Coinbase/Kraken BTC wallet and select "send", then in the "recipient" section copy the BTC address of the new exchange. Double check the amount of BTC you are sending, then click send and the transfer will initiate. Most of the time transfers take around 10 minutes, however, some exchanges take longer to process. Once your transfer is complete you can then exchange your BTC for any of the altcoins listed below.

Storing Your Coins - How to set up MyEtherWallet

Many of these coins are based on the Ethereum blockchain, and therefore use ERC20 tokens. Therefore, these tokens can be stored in Ethereum wallets. Wallets can be daunting to set up at first, so I recommend you use something simple to get started, the most convenient of these is MyEtherWallet.

Step-by-Step guide to setting up MyEtherWallet

1. Go to https://www.myetherwallet.com/

2. Enter a strong but easy to remember password. Do not forget it.

3. This encrypts (protects) your private key. It does not generate your private key. This password alone will not be enough to access your coins.

4. Click the "Generate Wallet" button.

5. Download your Keystore/UTC file & save this file to a USB drive.

6. This is the encrypted version of your private key. You need your password to access it. It is safer than your unencrypted private key but you must have your password to access it in the future.

7. Read the warning. If you understand it, click the "I understand. Continue" button.

8. Print your paper wallet backup and/or carefully hand-write the private key on a piece of paper.

9. If you are writing it, I recommend you write it 2 or 3 times. This decreases the chance your messy handwriting will prevent you from accessing your wallet later.

10. Copy & paste your address into a text document somewhere.

11. Search your address on https://etherscan.io/ Bookmark this page as this is how you can view your balance at any time

12. Send a small amount of any coin from your previous wallet or exchange to your new wallet - just to ensure you have everything correct

Hardware Wallets

Another safe, offline solution is to use a hardware wallet. The most popular of these being Trezor and Nano S. Both of these cost around $100, but represent a convenient, yet safe way to store your cryptocurrency. Further explanation of hardware wallets is in my first book *Cryptocurrency: Beginners Bible*.

10 High Potential Coins Under $1

Ambrosus (AMB)

Price at Time of Writing - $0.55

Market Cap at Time of Writing - $80,288,043

Available on:

BTC: Binance, Kucoin, Livecoin

ETH: Binance, Kucoin, RightBTC

Where to store:

AMB tokens are ERC20 tokens so you can store them in MyEtherWallet or other Ethereum wallets.

Ambrosus is another supply chain cryptocurrency project. This time based out of Switzerland and focused on two main market sectors, namely food and medicine. One of the core technology partners for the Ambrosus project is Parity Technologies.

By using real time sensors, linked to a blockchain, the project promises to monitor the distribution and food and medicine across the entire supply chain network. This will allow for anti-tampering monitoring as well as the enforcement of smart contracts to ensure the product reaches its end destination and an automatic payment is released based on the fulfillment of certain conditions.

For example, if you have a certain food that requires specific temperature, humidity and PH conditions to be met during transportation, a tracking device with a sensor that monitors these would be implemented in the container used to transport the goods. If all conditions are met when it reaches its end destination, then payment would automatically be released. If any of the conditions fail, the recipient would be notified in real time, and thus action could be taken accordingly.

There is also the issue of data storage, a blockchain solution means the data is publicly viewable so there are no issues regarding fraud, data hacking or manipulation.

Ambrosus' main asset at this time is the team behind its development. I would go as far as saying this is the best crypto development for a low market cap coin that I've seen in a long time. Headed up by CEO Angel Versetti, who has a wide industry background including time spent working at the United Nations, where he was the youngest project leader in UN history, and the World Resources Forum. He also has a corporate background with both financial firm Bloomberg and technology giant Google. CTO Dr. Stefan Meyer has a vast supply chain and food industry background having previously led R&D projects at Swiss food giant Nestle. The rest of the team is made up of equal parts storied corporate history and successful blockchain developers. They are backed up with some world class advisors including Oliver Bussman, previously named CTO of The Year by the Wall Street Journal. As well as Prof. Malcolm J W Povey, one of Britain's leading experts in food sensor technology. In a world of fake bio pictures, and develop aliases, a team as open and transparent with a history like this is frankly unprecedented in any but the biggest cryptocurrency projects.

Like many cryptocurrency projects, the Ambrosus project is built using the Ethereum blockchain.

So how is the token valuable? One of the biggest reasons for the low price right now is that the token economics have not yet been finalized. The main usage for AMB will be to facilitate transactions in the Ambrosus network, like how ETH is used for Ethereum and Gas is used for Neo. There are talks of masternodes being available, so users could stake their AMB tokens to help run the network and receive dividends in return. There are current debates about whether there would be larger funds needed to run a node or smaller funds with a legal contract. The alternative for this would be a two tier system with masternodes running alongside peer nodes.

In terms of competitors, there are a number of companies and crypto projects in the supply chain space. Two of the bigger ones out of China are VeChain and WaltonChain. WaltonChain is an RFID centered project, so the two may not be directly comparable. RFID is a limited technology that is pretty much limited to one (albeit important) function. However, with sensor technology, Ambrosus has a much larger usage scope. For example, the ability to monitor temperature and humidity. The project could be compared to Modum in this respect.

Where Ambrosus may be able to win though is the Swiss factor. It is much easier for European companies to do business with a fellow European company than it is for them to deal with Chinese ones. There is also the legitimacy issue. Will a company needing specialized supply chain solutions opt for a partnership with a Swiss company, in a country that has a long standing history of quality and impartiality. Or a Chinese company with a previous history of manipulation, in the case of WaltonChain's fake social media giveaway scandal. Getting first mover advantage and partnerships with large companies is going to be huge in which one of these supply chain projects has the highest ceiling, but Ambrosus certainly has a geographical advantage over its competitors in this respect.

Overall, this is certainly a long-term project with potential industry leading ramifications. As such, I wouldn't expect any giant price movements in the coming months. But as we move forward into 2019, there could well be big things for the Ambrosus project.

Jibrel Network (JNT)

Price at Time of Writing - $0.47

Market Cap at Time of Writing - $71,386,200

Available on:

BTC: Bibox, HitBTC, Gate.io

ETH: Bibox, HitBTC, Gate.io

Where to store:

JNT tokens are ERC20 tokens and thus can be stored using MyEtherWallet or by using a Ledger Nano S.

An interesting project based out of Switzerland that aims to bridge the gap between cryptocurrency and traditional markets. Jibrel focuses on government backed cryptocurrencies, so cryptocurrencies issued by central banks, but that still are backed by blockchain technology. You can think of Jibrel as a "decentral bank" in this respect.

The reason for the project is that while blockchain technology is an incredibly useful innovation, it is still limited in real world implementation due to the lack of widespread adoption for cryptocurrency. Co-Founder Yazan Barghuti summed this up well by saying "People pay their bills, their loans, and their mortgages in dollars, Euros, and pounds. They don't pay them in ETH or BTC."

So by bridging the gap, and implementing smart contracts with non-cryptocurrency based currencies, it will allow optimized real world transactions. For example, if a smart contract had been implemented on sub-prime loans and ratings before the 2008 financial crisis, we could have seen adjustments made prior to the market crash based on the actual performance and makeup of these assets, rather than outside pressure which forced ratings agencies to keep these bonds at a AAA rating. This is just one of the wide ranging theoretical applications of the Jibrel Network project.

Barghuti argues that the end user doesn't necessarily need to know their money is backed by cryptocurrency. They would want to use it the same way they always have. Similar to how online banking doesn't change the currency you are using, it's just backed by a computer instead of a bank book.

How Jibrel plans to do this is by using what it calls CryptoDepository Receipts or CryDRs. This will allow traditional financial assets to be backed by the Jibrel Network's cryptography. So if you held $100 in silver, for example, a USD CryDR would back this up with $100 worth of JNT tokens. These CryDRs could also be used for trading.

As far as the user side of things goes, Jibrel aims to make things simple and this is where the jWallet and jCash make their mark. jWallet will function as a regular cryptocurrency wallet, but aims to bring greater security to the equation. You can also use the wallet to exchange cryptocurrency for fiat currency the same way you would do so on an exchange. This can help protect your assets if you are worried about cryptocurrency volatility.

Initially, the project will run using the Ethereum network. It is interesting to note that all jWallet's will run using Jibrel's own Ethereum nodes, so the end user doesn't have to connect themselves. While some may argue that this is a centralized model, one which cryptocurrency purists often fight against - there are practical implications for this. Barghuti argues that this approach is one that favors scalability more than anything else, stating "'Yeah, but the whole point about Bitcoin is it's off-grid, etc.' Okay you can stay off-grid, and that's a $500 billion market. But if you go on-grid, you can start tackling the issues with the $34 trillion global economy."

Initially, Jibrel will support 6 fiat currencies and 2 further money market instruments, with plans to roll out further currencies in the future. Ultimately it would seem that support for 20 or 30 currencies at the same time would be completely possible.

In terms of the team behind it. Co-Founders Yazan Burghati and Talal Tabbaa both have a strong financial services background, both having previously worked for the Big 4 firms. The technical chops come from Victor Mezrin, who previously ran one of the largest altcoin mining operations in the world.

Going forward, we have the release of the Jibrel institutional level banking platform scheduled for Q3 2018. This will be a big determinant of whether the project is successful or not. There are very few cryptocurrency projects this close to launching such a significant venture, and if it is successful in the early stages, I doubt that Jibrel will stay at its current price. The only competitor coin I can think of who are targeting financial institutions on this scale would be QASH, based out of Japan, who I covered in a previous book.

Then in Q4, the team has planned the full scale launch of the decentralized Jibrel Network. By this time we will have a solid grasp of whether the project is going to be a smash hit, or if it will fall by the wayside. Like any project that deals with banks, licensing is going to be a tricky hurdle to overcome. Different countries have different licensing procedures which take different lengths of time to pass - and we've seen how this can delay projects in the past in the case of debit card projects like Monaco.

Either way, Jibrel Network is an extremely exciting project which huge ramifications if it is successful. A breath of fresh air in the sense that it addresses the current limitations of blockchain technology and aims to give real world application without needing to reinvent the wheel. I wouldn't expect too much price movement in the next quarter, but by the end of the year, we will have a better idea of just how successful the project can be.

LoMoCoin (LMC)

Price at Time of Writing - $0.07

Market Cap at Time of Writing - $18,033,963

Available on:

BTC: Bittrex, CoinExchange

Where to store:

The native LoMo app has a built in cryptocurrency wallet

LoMoCoin, also known as LoMoStar is an intriguing project out of China that focuses on the incentivized shopping space.

First and foremost to truly understand the potential of the coin, you must understand the market it is targeting. Incentivized shopping, in other words, shopping via the use of digital coupons, is a huge deal in China and across Asia. Many businesses have social media accounts, for example on WeChat, China's biggest smartphone social media platform, in which they distribute coupons directly to customers. In other words, if you want to go to Dunkin Donuts, for example, you can follow their WeChat account and you will receive a coupon for doing so. As businesses compete for foot traffic, coupon based shopping is becoming more popular than ever.

The concept centers around the Chinese tradition of "red envelopes". Traditionally these are given out on special occasions like Chinese New Year and contain money. With LoMo, these envelopes would be in the form of discount codes for local stores.

For example, you are out shopping with friends, when suddenly you get a notification on your phone notifying you of a flash sale in a nearby store. This store might even be one of your favorites, and thus you've just scored a huge discount. From the store's perspective, performing airdrops like these builds brand loyalty, and gives them a chance to win new business that they would not previously have had access to.

LoMoStar is the app itself that the currency is distributed through. The app promises to be an all-in-one shopping and social platform where users can not only claim rewards and spend their cryptocurrency, but also perform their own airdrops with their friends. The app also has a built in cryptocurrency exchange, which while not revolutionary, will be convenience once increased adoption continues.

This kind of native advertising brings disruption to the traditional model of sponsored ads like Google AdWords and Facebook Ads. Year by year these are representing lower returns for those using them, as ad price increases and customers get more and more "overmarketed". In other words, they make a lot of money for Google and Facebook, but often represent poor ROI for the businesses running the ads.

The main driving force behind LoMo is the number of users downloading the app itself. As the user base becomes bigger, more businesses have incentives to do airdrops, and thus we can see somewhat of a snowball effect. Having a low barrier to entry "on-ramp" so to speak is a great way to attract those who are new to the cryptocurrency space. We have seen this in the past with coins like Ripple that became "accessible" due to their low price, despite their high market cap and limited room for growth going forward. Being able to take your first step into the crypto world just by downloading a smartphone app is a very simple solution for many users. Especially in target areas like Shanghai as well as other large Asian cities like Tokyo and Seoul.

Many users have reported earning over $100 USD worth of coins within the first few months of having the app on their phones. Which isn't bad seeing as you don't really have to do anything to get them. You can then transfer these tokens to more established cryptocurrencies like Bitcoin and Ethereum if you wish. Once again, this just reiterates the low barrier to entry effect and how this could be a huge bonus going forward.

The big question with this project is the same question we have with any project based in China. There is a certain risk involved with Chinese companies due to the cultural and regulatory differences when compared to the West. This is then compounded by the Chinese government's reactionary stance on cryptocurrency and often sweeping change in the law. For example, one of the biggest events in 2017 was when the government decided that Chinese citizens could not participate in ICOs, which led to a big downturn in the market. What further compounded this drop is that many media outlets in the West reported this event as "China bans cryptocurrency."

In terms of the team, I have to say I was very impressed. There are over 70 employees, many of whom have a solid blockchain background. CEO Xiong LiJian was previously involved in Litecoin mining development on both the hardware and software side.

Then we have to examine the potential for the project outside of China. Although the app currently has airdrops in multiple countries, it remains to be seen just how widespread adoption will be outside of the Middle Kingdom. That said, even if the idea is *only* successful within China, there will still be significant growth from the current price.

Overall, I like the idea of LoMo and their app. The social element could play a big part in bringing new users into the cryptocurrency space, which is vital if the technology is going to grow as we move forward. Low barriers to entry combined with incentivized rewards for using it, mean we could see industry changing ramifications. These are still early days, but if you are interested and want to see for yourself just how the project works, I recommend downloading the app on your iPhone or Android and check it out. After all, if you aren't yet invested in crypto, this could be your first chance to own coins of your very own, without having to invest a single penny.

WePower (WPR)

Price at Time of Writing - $0.17

Market Cap at Time of Writing - $60,534,439

Available on:

BTC: Huobi, Liqui

ETH: Huobi, Liqui

Where to store:

WePower is an ERC20 token and can by stored in MyEtherWallet

An eco-friendly blockchain solution that focuses on the renewable energy sector. By creating a platform that allows green energy producers to interact with energy investors and green energy consumers, they have an incentive to keep creating renewable energy sources. For consumers, they would be able to purchase energy directly at a rate below the market price due to the lack of need for a middleman such as a government body. The project has already been listed as one of the Top 10 innovative energy initiatives in Europe by Fast Company magazine. The size of the renewable energy sector is growing every year with an estimated $200 billion of new investment annually. The team estimates the token market potential to be approximately $1.2 trillion per year.

By using blockchain technology and smart contract implementation, the project solves compliance issues such as a green energy owner selling energy that isn't theirs for example.

The tokens themselves will be tied to energy prices, and thus will naturally be more stable than other cryptocurrencies. This is important when we ask the question of "why can't the project just use BTC or ETH for transactions". By running the platform like this, it gives an inherent need for the WPR token and thus the WPR token itself has an intrinsic value, which is a big part of any cryptocurrency project.

The platform will use an auction model, in which producers put their tokens up for sale and buyers have 48 hours to bid on them. After these 48 hours have expired, non-token holders have the opportunity to buy them as well. This unique approach to trading green energy gives WePower a huge first mover advantage when it comes to the energy trading sector, particularly in the eco-friendly part of it.

The project's initial focus will be on the European market because EU member states all share a common energy agreement with regards to regulations. This agreement makes cross border energy trading relatively seamless. The project is currently in talks with the Lithuanian government about a joint venture with nationalized energy companies. Pilot projects are also underway in Estonia.

The renewable energy sector is one that continues to receive a lot of government support, for both blockchain and non-blockchain ventures. This support could be huge for WePower when we compare it to other cryptocurrencies projects that often run into red tape and bureaucracy. Having backing from a government, rather than having to fight it, will be vital if the project is to succeed.

In terms of the team behind the project, Co-Founder Nikolaj Martyniuk has over 10 years experience in the green energy sector. He is backed up by team members with FinTech backgrounds, energy consultants and blockchain experts.

Progress has been solid so far and a demo platform is already available on the WePower website for users to test out.

A big step for the project came in late February 2018 when it was announced that Binance included WePower in the latest round of voting for inclusion on the platform. This is a community poll where Binance members can vote on coins they want to see included on the platform. If the coin wins the poll then it will be included on Binance for trading. Early results indicate that the coin has been doing well in the polls and at the time of writing ranked number 2 behind Dentacoin.

Going forward, there are a number of near future dates on the roadmap that you need to be aware of. April 2018 will see a full scale testing of the project in Estonia, if this is successful then it will no doubt mean big things for the project. Especially in a space where many crypto projects are still firmly in the theoretical stage. Later testing is scheduled for Q4 2018 in Spain and Australia. The first actual distributed energy will be in December 2018. Then there are further expansion plans for 2019.

Overall, I like the approach of the project with the token system being particularly appealing. The idea of a green energy trading platform without middlemen is a fantastic application of blockchain technology. The need for the WPR token is another huge plus that just can't be overlooked. Listing on a larger exchange will be key in the short term, but the real challenge will be seeing if the testing phases in Estonia, Spain and Australia are successful. If they are, then this coin won't stay this low for long.

TheKey (TKY)

Price at Time of Writing - $0.0187

Market Cap at Time of Writing - Currently unknown due to lack of concrete information about circulating market supply. Based on estimated supply of 3.63 billion, we can make an approximate market cap estimation of around $65,000,000.

Available on:

BTC: Kucoin

ETH: Kucoin

NEO: Kucoin

Where to store:

TheKey uses the Neo protocol (NEP5) and thus you can store it in a Neo wallet. You can download one from the official Neo website https://neo.org/download - desktop, mobile and web wallets are available

Another project coming out of China, TheKey aims to use blockchain technology to create a decentralized national identification system.

This has many different uses in practical terms. One of the main ones being in healthcare. For example, individual citizens could apply for a smart identification card which would be linked to their cellphone. They could then use this to book doctor's appointments online. When they arrive at the hospital, the doctor could have automatic access to their medical records, and their insurance details. The ID could also be linked to a payment method, which could automatically pay for any medical bills required.

This then has anti-fraud ramifications, which could be useful for things like automatically ordering medication. For example, elderly patients could have medicine delivered to their home, so they wouldn't have to leave the house in order to get necessary medicines. Currently, there is no system in place which allows them to do this, because of concerns about people stealing identities to order medicine in order to resell it on the black market.

One of the first ICOs to use the Neo platform rather than Ethereum. ONCHAIN, the company behind Neo is also listed as a strategic partner for the project. The ICO itself was not without problems, as it went live at 2AM CET, which was immediately followed by a website crash and the donation amounts being filled without any chance for European investors to take part.

The coin boasts a number of big partnerships with Chinese companies, namely AliPay (AliBaba's payment platform). There are also plans to trial the technology in two pilot cities, with Jiaxing being the first one.

15 different patents have already been awarded by the Chinese State Intellectual Property Office (SIPO) which is promising to see and shows that the project clearly aims to have a larger scope than others.

The project is headed up by Catherine Li, who boasts an incredibly strong track record of entrepreneurship within China. In 2017 she was awarded Most Outstanding Women Entrepreneurs in China by the All-China Women's Federation. She previously worked at IMS Health, which provides big data solutions in the healthcare space. She is backed up by blockchain lead Ken Huang who worked at phone manufacturer Huawei as a Chief Blockchain Developer.

In terms of competition, the biggest project would be Civic. However, TheKey's focus on China is what makes it stand out. Chinese governments tend to favor internal projects rather than international ones. And if TheKey can garner some early adoption within China, this will make any nationwide or international rollout much easier. This is what sets it apart from the other identity verification blockchain projects. The other factor to remember, especially for a project like this, is that there doesn't only have to be "one winner", many competing projects can and will co-exist side by side, and take up a decent market share.

In terms of roadmap, the project mainnet is scheduled for release in December of 2018.

Right now the low price can be attributed to overall market conditions and lack of listing on a larger exchange. Kucoin is fairly solid and reliable but there just isn't the volume of a Binance or a Bittrex to support higher prices. A March announcement that the coin would be listed on Chinese exchange LBank, which is currently the 16th largest exchange in the world by volume, so this could have some additional growth effects in the short term.

The other drawback is the lack of literature available about the project in English. After studying the official website for some time, I still had a number of unanswered questions that I had to go to unofficial sources within the community to find the answers to. Once greater clarification is made in English on the official website, I have no doubt that more investors will be attracted to the project.

Out of all the projects I've discussed in this book, I'd say this is no doubt one of the more high-risk, high-reward type projects. The Chinese factor, and lack of English communication does mean we could all be mislead into believing the project is further along than it is. However, if you are willing to accept this, this could well be one of the biggest gainers of 2018 and beyond. From a blockchain enthusiast standpoint, it's interesting to see how scalable a NEP5 token will be when compared to one running on the Ethereum network. If TheKey fits your risk/reward profile then it is definitely a project worth checking out.

Note: The project is not to be confused with KeyCoin or SelfKey, which both use the (KEY) symbol.

SelfKey in particular focuses on the same space so please ensure you are buying the correct token.

Oyster Pearl (PRL)

Price at Time of Writing - $0.97

Market Cap at Time of Writing - $72,546,189

Available on:

BTC: Kucoin, Cryptopia

ETH: Kucoin, CoinExchange, IDEX

NEO: Kucoin

Where to store:

PRL Tokens can be stored in MyEtherWallet. To create a custom token take the following steps.

Contract Address: 0x1844b21593262668B7248d0f57a220CaaBA46ab9
Symbol: PRL
Decimals: 18

Oyster Pearl addresses the issue of advertising on websites and provides a solution that satisfies both business owners and consumers who are browsing the websites. In their own words "Goodbye banner ads. Hello Oyster." The project combines decentralized storage and payment for content creators.

Currently, it is estimated that 50% of web users have some sort of ad blocking software installed on their computer or on their browser. Much of the other 50% have become somewhat immune to ads due to their frequency.

How it works is by using web visitors' excess computing power (CPU and GPU power) to store files on a decentralized ledger. This excess power provides Proof of Work which maintains the storage network. Site owners are then paid by the storage users, and in turn, web visitors get an ad-free browser experience.

The files themselves are stored on the IOTA tangle and uses Ethereum smart contracts in order to verify correct storage data. Because of all the data is encrypted and decentralized, fragments of files are stored rather than complete ones, this makes the files more secure than if they were stored on a centralized server like Dropbox for example. This model is open source, so the community can monitor it and ensure there is no nefarious action occurring at any time.

The project makes it extremely simple for businesses to adopt. In fact, all you need to do is add a single line of HTML code to your existing website. So any website that can run Javascript, can run the Oyster protocol. In theory, this should also provide little to no browser slow down or impacted computer performance on the user end either. This simplicity is quite remarkable in a space where many blockchain projects require developers to learn entirely new programming languages just to take advantage of a particular project.

There are a number of blockchain cloud storage projects, with a chief competitor being Storj, which is built entirely on the Ethereum blockchain. However, the main difference between the two is that Storj is strictly focused on storage, without the advertising incentives given to website owners. Siacoin is another competitor, although that project has run into numerous difficulties since their ICO last year. Oyster also has no plans to charge fees for downloading any stored files, whereas Sia does charge per download.

The team is headed up by anonymous developer Bruno Block. This person's anonymity is a cause for concern for some investors, while others are less worried about it. I should say that developers wishing to remain anonymous, while strange, is not uncommon in the crypto space. Much of the other team has come forward with their identities, and maintain public LinkedIn profiles. CTO Alex Firmani has a solid background in the cloud storage space, so industry experience is there. Many of the engineers on the project also have active GitHub profiles which is promising to see.

The main areas to monitor going forward are adoption. Will websites actually use the Oyster protocol versus the traditional advertising models like Google AdSense? Another area of caution would be whether the code added to the HTML will flag a site a malicious by certain anti-virus and anti-malware software.

A more technical concern would be the scalability of IOTA's Tangle network, which at this point has yet to be tested. The Oyster team have already said they will move to their own blockchain solution if the Tangle cannot live up to their needs. This is fine in theory, however, in practice, any switch will have a significant impact on the project.

In terms of roadmap, the team are currently in the Testnet A stage of thins, with Testnet B scheduled for later this year. Testnet B will be a public testnet. Mainnet is currently scheduled for April 2018 which is when Oyster will be fully up and running, and tweaks can be made if necessary.

Oyster Pearl tokens (PRL) are ERC20 tokens. After the latest coin burn there are around 98 million tokens in circulation. The token will be used to pay website owners who install the Oyster code on their site.

If you can overlook an anonymous figure heading the project up, Oyster Pearl is an ambitious project with great potential. Seeing a project running on IOTA's tangle is great to see from an adoption standpoint, and this is certainly a coin to look at closely.

ChainLink (LINK)

Price at Time of Writing - $0.51

Market Cap at Time of Writing - $179,183,250

Available on:

BTC: Binance, Huobi, OKEx

ETH: Binance, Huobi, OKEx

Where to store:

LINK tokens are ERC 20 tokens and can by stored on MyEtherWallet or other Ethereum wallets.

Based out of the US, ChainLink is one of the more ambitious projects out there and aims to create a platform where users can attach smart contracts to existing apps and data. This acts as a bridge between non-blockchain resources like bank accounts and data services and a public smart contract ledger. This would allow users to create contracts that perform the same function as real world binding agreements, but without the expensive middleman.

The entire theory behind the project is that current smart contract platform does not function with off-chain resources. Therefore a bridge is needed and that's where ChainLink comes into play. By acting as a bridge, the contract can be verified on the blockchain, without the data feeds needing to be on that blockchain as well.

In terms of use cases, there are many. For example, say you own a large warehouse that stores valuable goods. These goods are stolen one night, and you need to make an insurance claim. However, the insurance company is pushing back by claiming that the magnetic doors to the warehouse may not have been locked and thus this represents user error. By using ChainLink to connect the monitoring data for the doors, with your insurance contract - you would have an undisputed answer to the question. The same goes for an issue like a payment for a delayed flight, using ChainLink you have publicly verifiable data about how late the flight arrived and for what reason.

Maybe the biggest real world use case is in financial reporting. This could be anything from bond rates, interest rates and other derivatives. ChainLink would allow users to connect to external networks (like Bloomberg) in order to verify the correct data and thus the contract would pay out accordingly.

One of the bigger factors ChainLink has going for it is the ability to let users settle contracts in both fiat currency and LINK tokens. This will no doubt help real world adoption of the technology. The team even discusses this on their website and states that the current limitation of other smart contract platforms to mimic real-world financial agreements. As we saw int he case of the Jibrel Network, in the short to medium term, we will need some sort of bridging between traditional finance and cryptocurrency before we see widespread adoption of cryptocurrency only platforms.

The platform currently has partnerships in place with a number of other smart contract firms including zeppelin_os which powers over $1.5 billion worth of smart contracts. Another agreement is in place with Cornell University's Town Crier initiative - a patent pending system which verifies the security and trustworthiness of data.

An agreement is also in place with the payment network SWIFT. This came after the team won the Innotribe Industry Challenge in 2016. They are now working with SWIFT to develop a Proof of Concept - this will be centered around LINK smart contracts verified interest rates across data sources in order to generate a LIBOR average rate. The smart contract will then be used to generate secure payments based on this rate.

The main things holding back the project right now are the small development team. For the first 3 years of the project, there were only two developers, although CEO Sergey Nazarov confirmed at the end of 2017 that they had hired more members. Lack of updates from the team has been an issue, and a lack of public roadmap is also a cause for concern. For a project as mature as this one, greater public visibility is needed in the short term to reassure investors that everything is moving forward as they would have hoped.

In terms of the token itself. There are 1 billion LINK tokens in circulation, of which 350 million are in the current circulating supply. The team holds 30% with the other 70% split between Node Operators (needed to upkeep the network) and the general public. One interesting thing to note is that unlike other projects, there is no minimum staking requirement to become a node operator. Therefore this allows any users to participate in the network and earns passive income for doing so. Although the payout structure is yet to be finalized, this is certainly something to be aware of if you are interested in staking coins but don't have a huge amount of them.

Overall, ChainLink is a solid project that has proven real world application already. The partnerships in place are impressive, and the only thing holding it back is lack of transparency from the team. I would like to see them hire a full time press officer and marketing manager in order to better communicate the progress going forward. However, the technology alone makes this project well worth looking into.

SONM (SNM)

Price at Time of Writing - $0.15

Market Cap at Time of Writing - $54,959,826

Available on:

BTC: Binance, Tidex, Liqui

ETH: Binance, Liqui, Kucoin

Where to store:

SNM tokens are ERC 20 tokens and can by stored on MyEtherWallet or other Ethereum wallets.

SONM is a fascinating supercomputer project powered by the Ethereum blockchain, powered by miners using their idle computer resources. The project has already received some decent mainstream media attention and was voted #6 on the Top 10 Blockchain Projects To Watch Out For in 2018 by EntreprenEuros Magazine.

This has tremendous application including everything from web hosting to mobile and web applications, machine learning, scientific research, servers for hosting video games and video streaming.

This represents advantages to those needing to use these services when compared to the standard centralized solutions that we see today. Because the rental time on the supercomputer is completely flexible with no minimum amounts or minimum contract lengths - buyers only pay for the exact amount they need to use. If the task then takes fewer resources than the buyer anticipated, they will be refunded for the resources they did not need.

Miners have an incentive for powering the network as they will be paid in SNM tokens. You don't have to have a super powerful computer either, you can use your regular desktop or laptop. You can even use other devices with internet capabilities like your XBox and even your cellphone. Originally there were plans for SNM token holders to be rewarded with the network fees from the project, although this was dismissed due to potential regulatory issues (as the token would then be deemed a "security" by the SEC). There are still plans to reward token holders, but the economics have yet to be finalized. This isn't a major issue at this early stage, but it would be nice to see some additional information about this from the team within the next 6 months.

The project can be looked at as similar to Golem (GNT) which I discussed in the first edition of Cryptocurrency: Insider Secrets. Both aim to use idle computer resources to power supercomputers and thus we can view them as direct competitors. The one advantage SONM does have is that it plans to use the supercomputer for a wider variety of applications than just GPU rendering like the Golem project. In terms of development, SONM also has the advantage being further ahead on its roadmap. Once again, we should restate that there's no reason these two projects can co-exist with equal market shares.

Both projects share the same growing pains, namely, can the Ethereum network handle the sheer volume of transactions required to run a supercomputer like this. SONM's solution is to build their own sidechain (essentially an additional blockchain) which will process some of the transactions and lower the overall load on the Ethereum network. This sidechain will reduce all internal transaction costs to zero.

SONM has already announced a partnership with fellow Ethereum project Storj (discussed in Ethereum: Beginners Bible), the decentralized cloud storage platform. This will allow users to share files on the SONM platform. This additional step towards fully decentralized cloud computing is certainly an achievement going forward. Plus, it is always good to see blockchain project working together in order to gain mainstream adoption.

March brought news of another partnership, this time with blockchain AI platform DBrain. DBrain will be utilizing SONM's supercomputer to convert raw data into real world AI solutions for businesses around the world. SONM CEO Alexei Antonov stated, "Collaboration with Dbrain is an excellent way of demonstrating the possibilities of our project."

One thing SONM does extremely well is hitting their roadmap deadlines. From my research, I found they consistently hit project advancements on or before they were scheduled to. This demonstrates consistency from the team, and adds an extra layer of trustworthiness that other cryptocurrency projects simply do not have. Trust is vital in a space where the early years were dominated by news of theft, hackings and criminal activity.

As previously mentioned, users can buying resources using the SNM token, and those donating their idle computing power will be paid using the token as well. This already gives the token an intrinsic value, and use case - which is always one thing to look for when examining cryptocurrency projects.

In terms of roadmap, an MVP was released in late 2017 and a successful bug bounty round (rewarding users for finding bugs or errors in the code) occurred after that. A Windows client was also launched around this time. The first fee payouts are scheduled for Q2 2018. Followed by a full network release along with the full version of the SONM wallet on the Ethereum network - which is scheduled for July-August 2018.

In the short term, continued announcements of collaborations with other companies will be key to driving price action. In terms of growth potential, Golem currently has a market cap 6X higher than SONM's, and while the project is more mature, it seems that the SONM team are moving forward at a faster rate. This is one of the projects in the book that could have significant price action on both a short and long term basis.

OriginTrail (TRAC)

Price at Time of Writing - $0.18

Market Cap at Time of Writing - $48,535,364

Available on:

ETH: IDEx, HitBTC, ForkDelta

Where to store:

TRAC tokens are ERC 20 tokens and can by stored in MyEtherWallet and other Ethereum wallets.

OriginTrail is a blockchain project that focuses on the supply chain sector. The project was developed in order to combat the scalability problems that other decentralized supply chain projects are facing. The project has already won a number of plaudits in the industry including Walmart China's Food Safety Innovation and the Food + City People's Choice Award.

Supply chain data is often fragmented, as it comes from multiple different sources. This makes it difficult to track and monitor. OriginTrail aims to make this data more manageable without slowing down the process. You could potentially use this to track foos deliveries and authenticity of products when looking at their labels among other things. For example, a 2017 study showed to 70% of wine sold in China was fake. Meaning that it's origins were not what was stated on the bottle and was instead a mix of cheaper wine and water. This fake wine is then sold at a huge markup, which is often over 1000%. There have also been stories of rice contamination across the country. Another investigation, this time by the Wall Street

Journal indicated that over one third of the fish sold in the United States was mislabeled. Needless to say, the current solutions are not offering the level of transparency that consumers require.

One very important thing to note is that the OriginTrail network can function across different blockchain protocols. This is known in the industry as being "blockchain agnostic". So it can be used in conjunction with projects built on Ethereum, Neo and IOTA for example, rather than just being limited to one of these at a time. This cross-operability is a huge step in any blockchain project, let alone one that has a lot of potential adoption like the supply chain sector. This would also allow large institutions (like Walmart for example) to build their own blockchain solutions and OriginTrail would be compatible with these. This could also potentially lead to partnerships with some of the biggest players in the industry.

This has many different applications across the sector including product authentication, supply chain management and food journey visibility. As well as backend functions like inventory management and production alert systems.

This is not a new initiative, and the core team has been performing supply chain tracing since 2013. However, they only began implementing blockchain technology in 2016.

The coin is backed up by a solid development team, each with a visible public profile on LinkedIn and extensive industry experience. Co-Founders Tomaz Levak and Ziga Drev both having backgrounds in supply chain management and tracing supply chains in Eurosope and the Middle East.

In terms of token use, TRAC tokens are a necessity for the network to function. The tokens are used to create nodes that hold up the network and process data transactions. Those who run nodes will be rewarded in the form of TRAC tokens. It is not yet confirmed if the project will use masternodes, and if so, how much these will be. Nor has any potential reward amount been confirmed yet. If you do have enough TRAC tokens to run a masternode, this would represent a fantastic passive income opportunity.

In terms of roadmap, the beta version of the testnet is currently scheduled for June. This will be the iron out any kinks and test OriginTrail's applications in various environments. After this, the mainnet is planned for Q3 2018 release.

Lack of a big exchange is the big thing holding back the price as of now. Not only are they not on the bigger exchanges like Binance or Bittrex, there aren't even any coin pairings on an exchange I would consider "mid-level" at this point.

OriginTrail is one of those cryptocurrency projects with industry changing ramifications IF they can achieve widespread adoption. It's a big if, as supply chain management is arguably the most competitive of the cryptocurrency project niches. However, their blockchain agnostic design may well be the "killer application" of this particular project. The ability to work with both open source and private blockchains is simply too be to be ignored, and thus this makes OriginTrail a project well worth looking into.

Note: BTC/TRAC trading is available on CoinFalcon (not to be confused with scam crypto lending platform Falcon Coin) - but the volume available is so low (<$1000 daily) I have not formally included it

Mercury Protocol (GMT)

Price at Time of Writing - $0.02

Market Cap at Time of Writing - $4,420,198

Available on:

ETH: ForkDelta

Where to store:

GMT tokens are ERC 20 tokens and can be stored in MyEtherWallet and other Ethereum wallets

By far the smallest crypto project discussed in this book, with a market cap of just under $4.5 million, Mercury Protocol is a decentralized communication platform. The project itself has been around for over 4 years, with blockchain implementation starting in 2016. On the website, Mercury Protocol lists famed billionaire Mark Cuban as an advisor. Cuban is an investor in Radical App LLC, the parent company behind the project.

The reasoning behind the project is that the current messaging model is centralized and relies on selling user data to advertisers for profit.

The platform offers demographic targeting as well, so advertisers can focus in on their audience, without wasting money by sending announcements to those who are not interested in what they are selling.

The main question you may be asking yourself at this point is - why would someone use Mercury Protocol built apps over other messaging apps that have their own internal economy such as WeChat? The answer to this is that GMT tokens are transferable across different Mercury Protocol apps. The theory behind this is that by allowing use across multiple platforms, it will create a network effect that will expand the user base and encourage widespread adoption. To give an example, imagine if there was a single token you could use on Facebook, Instagram, Whatsapp and Slack - this would be rather handy for both advertisers and users alike.

There are plans to make the entire platform open source in future released, so developers may then be able to make modifications and find any code bugs. There are concerns that this would lead to the rise of "clone platforms" - however, any clone platforms would need a large user base themselves to benefit from this.

GMT or Global Messaging Tokens can be used by network providers to make announcements on the network. The wider audience you want to make an announcement to, the more tokens it will cost. Users could be rewarded with tokens for watching adverts as well, which encourages them to use the platform in the first place. The team also believes that these tokens can incentivize good behavior on the platform and be used to eliminate trolling and online bullying. For example, users will be deducted tokens for harassment. The use of GMT versus BTC or ETH was done to minimize volatility from external factors. For example, if you buy a premium message with 1 ETH, then the price of ETH rises because of unrelated news, then you have just lost out. By using GMT, the price is generally only affected by activity within the Mercury Protocol network.

The token supply is fixed, so there is no mining involved. Users can earn more tokens by participating in the apps themselves.

In terms of roadmap, the mainnet release of the Dust app, the first built on the protocol, is scheduled for Q1 2018. You can download the beta version right now from the App Store or Google Play Store if you want to check it out for yourself. A second app known as Broadcast is currently in development.

The primary concern right now is the complete lack of any marketing effort from the core team. I understand they are working hard on the platform itself, but personally I believe that a coin should always be marketing itself, at least in order to stay relevant in a space that sees multiple projects pop up every day. Even a small weekly update on development progress would be a start. Once we move further into 2018, then talks of partnerships can be discussed and moved along.

In summary, this is no doubt a high risk project because of the small size and need for mass adoption to be successful. I think that it may see more success in niche markets rather than a full on social media 2.0 vision that some share. Even with niche market success though, there's no doubt the current token price and market cap would rise. They have a working product out which is a plus as well. All in all, for the low barrier to entry, it's a solid project with a lot of room to grow and should be looked at closely.

How to Buy Coins on Coinbase With Zero Transaction Fees

Please note: This method only works for countries eligible for Revolut bank accounts which include the USA, Canada and the UK.

If you haven't heard of Revolut, it's a digital bank based in the UK. There have free currency transfers among 26 currencies - which is how we can use this to our benefit. You can even open an account in less than 30 seconds by using the Revolut app.

This is beneficial for Coinbase users because you can save up to 4% on each transaction by doing this, so if you're heavily involved in crypto you can potentially save hundreds of dollars per year.

Now, onto how Revolut can help you save money on cryptocurrency transactions.

Step 1: Send your native currency like GBP or USD, to your Revolut account via debit card. This step is easy and Revolut walks you through it when you set up an account. This transfer should be near instant.

Step 2: Exchange your native fiat currency to Euros on Revolut. Revolut has no transaction fees for this, so you get the market rate.

Step 3: Bank transfer your Euros from Revolut to Coinbase. This is the only step which is not instant, it takes 1 business day, so if you do it before 3PM EST you should get your coins before 9AM the next morning.

Step 4: Once your Euros are in your Coinbase account, transfer them to your GDAX wallet from Coinbase. If you're not familiar with GDax, it is Coinbase's sister platform designed for traders. Transfer between Coinbase and GDax are instant and free.

Step 5: Buy your coins on GDAX using Euro pairings, making sure to use Limit orders instead of Market orders, as these are free. If you use market orders, you will pay a 0.25% transaction fee.

Step 6: Transfer your newly purchased coins from GDAX to a personal wallet, or another exchange like Binance.

A Brand New Way to Buy Cryptocurrency Which Could Have Huge Market Ramifications

March brought news of an exciting development for those of you who want to get involved in cryptocurrency, but don't want to go through the process of buying and storing coins yourself.

I should note at the outset, this method is not viable for those of you only looking to buy a small amount of coins. This is strictly reserved for this with a lot of cash to spend.

US exchange Coinbase announced that they would be beginning the Coinbase Index Fund, aimed at becoming the "Dow of Cryptocurrencies". The fund will automatically diversify your cryptocurrency portfolio and rebalance it on a monthly basis. In the beginning, the fund will feature Bitcoin, Ethereum, Litecoin and Bitcoin Cash, any new coins added to Coinbase will automatically be added to the fund.

In the beginning stages, the fund will be offered to accredited US investors with assets of more than $1 million. Eventually, the threshold will be lowered in stages until the minimum investment is $10,000. There are also plans to roll the fund out across other geographical markets. The fund will charge a 3% management fee, which on the surface seems high. However, if you are looking for a truly passive crypto asset, this may well tick all your boxes.

How does this benefit the rest of the market? Any kind of institutional adoption is a positive sign. Last year we had 2 different Bitcoin ETFs rejected by the SEC on volatility grounds, so this is the next best option in the interim.

Things You Need to Be Aware of With Certain Cryptocurrency Channels on YouTube

For those of your planning to do extra research before buying coins, which is something I always recommend - YouTube is a great place to start. Many content creators do an in-depth analysis of coins in a similar fashion to what I do here. However, there are certain red flags you should look out for when determining how reliable the information on a certain channel is.

The creator has been paid to advertise coins in the past

Many of these channels, especially the ones with larger followings, are paid by the cryptocurrency teams to advertise the coin on their channel. There is no inherent problem with this, after all, it is just a form of advertising. The problem lies where the creator does not disclose they received payment to discuss the coin. And instead disguises this analysis in the form of a supposedly unbiased review.

The creator uses high pressure sales tactics or fake scarcity

Language such as "this coin will go up any day now" or "get in fast before you miss out", designed to spark a fear of missing out among the viewer, are rife in the crypto space. If a channel discusses a coin's price moreso than the project or team behind it, then you must be skeptical. If you find a channel that does this, then you have to take their "advice" with a pinch of salt.

The creator does not disclose their current holdings

There's nothing wrong with cryptocurrency personalities having their own portfolio, however, they should disclose whether they own a coin or not before discussing it in a public space.

The big one: They make promises of guaranteed returns

This one is the biggest red flag. There is a huge difference between discussing projects with potential and promising guaranteed returns if you invest in a certain project. This often is associated with coin lending platforms, such as BitConnect and Davor Coin, both of which exit scammed and caused anyone invested in them to lost 95% of their money. Remember this moreso than anything else. **There is no such thing as guaranteed returns in any investment - cryptocurrency or otherwise.**

Note: While writing this book, another lending platform Falcon Coin performed an exit scam, leaving investors with 98% losses on their initial investment.

Conclusion

And that's it - 10 more exciting altcoins under $1 that have fantastic potential for gains in the next 12 months and beyond.

I hope this information has been beneficial to you and has given you a foundation to invest some of the more unknown cryptocurrencies. Even with the rocky start to the year, there has never been a more exciting time for cryptocurrencies than right now. Even if you missed the boat with coins like Neo and Stellar, it's not too late.

As always, I encourage you to do additional research before investing in any of these, particularly by checking out the white papers on the individual coin websites, which will give you a much more in-depth look at the technology behind them.

Remember to invest wisely, and always with your own money. Never borrow money to invest in cryptocurrency or anything else. For your own sanity, don't check your investments on a daily basis. This is a volatile market, and you have to be willing to accept that if you are to make long term profits. Perhaps most importantly, don't panic sell if you see a dip in the market. From a personal standpoint, if I had sold during the crash caused by the famous Mt. Gox incident, in which Bitcoin lost over 60% of its value - I would be a much poorer man than I am today.

I wish you the best of luck in the cryptocurrency market, and I hope you make a lot of money.

Thanks,

Stephen

Cryptocurrency: Mining for Beginners - How You Can Make Up To $18,500 a Year Mining Coins From Home

By Stephen Satoshi

Introduction

Welcome to the exciting world of cryptocurrency mining. First things first, congratulations on buying this book and thank you for doing so.

The following chapters will discuss in detail what exactly cryptocurrency mining is, how it works, and most importantly, different ways you can make a profit from mining cryptocurrency.

You'll learn about various mining techniques such as staking, pool mining, and rig mining. You'll also discover "outside the box" ways to profit from mining coins, some of which don't even require you to do any mining yourself. Of course, as is the case with all my books, we'll also be highlighting any cryptocurrency scams or schemes which I feel you should avoid as well.

These are truly exciting ways of earning coins without having to buy at the exchanges.

Finally, this book assumes you have little to no knowledge of cryptocurrency mining and how it all works, so the language is designed to be as easy to understand as possible.

I hope you enjoy the content of this book, and I wish you the best of your cryptocurrency journey.

Thanks,

Stephen

Basic Overview of Mining Cryptocurrencies

By now you probably already know a decent amount about cryptocurrencies. They are digital assets that function as a medium of exchange and use cryptography to secure transactions and to create additional units. Cryptocurrencies are mined into existence through a process known as mining. This process of mining new cryptocurrencies involves two functions. These are adding transactions to the blockchain and releasing new currency to the system.

Mining Cryptocurrencies

In order to mine cryptocurrencies, you need access to a powerful computer and special software. There are new, sophisticated computers in the market that have been developed specifically for cryptocurrency mining.

A miner is basically anyone who invests his or her time confirming cryptocurrency transactions and adding new currencies to its network. Mining cryptocurrency requires plenty of resources. The computers needed for this process are costly and operating costs are very high. This is because the mining process consumes a lot of electricity.

Miners generally spend most of their time trying to confirm a block containing data using hash functions. To understand better how the mining process works, it is important to first understand the basic aspects of blockchain technology.

Mining and the Blockchain

Cryptocurrencies use publicly distributed and decentralized ledgers known as blockchain. Blockchains are secure networks and this is in part due to the mining process. Mining is, therefore, an essential component of the blockchain and is integral to its stability. It provides an additional level of security because the process validates each transaction that takes place on the blockchain.

In fact, the validity of each cryptocurrency coin is secured by the blockchain. Each block contains what is known as a hash pointer. The blockchain is decentralized with no central server to log in all transactions. However, without sufficient computing power, the blockchain ledger cannot operate. Cryptocurrencies rely on the combined power of numerous mining computers spread out across the world.

These computers are operated by miners who lend their computers for a common cause. In return for their input, they receive an incentive or reward. Miners receive payment when they solve a challenging mathematical puzzle and validate transactions before others do.

Each block in the blockchain contains transaction data, a timestamp, and a hash pointer.

Hash Function

The hash function in cryptocurrency is an algorithm that maps data of varying or arbitrary size to a hash and is by design a one-way function. A hash pointer is present in all block and always points to the previous block. It acts as a pointer, making it easy to track transactions.

Proof of Work

Most of the blockchains in use today use a concept known as Proof of Work. Proof of Work protocol or system is simply an economic measure that requires some work from the requesters to be done. This work is often processing time by a computer. This helps prevent service abuse.

Proof of Work scheme is the first timestamping scheme that was invented for the blockchain. The most popular proof-of-work schemes are based on scrypt and SHA-256. Scrypt is the most widely used among cryptocurrencies. Others include SHA-3, Crypto-Night and Blake.

CPU versus GPU Mining

There are several options available when it comes to cryptocurrency mining. At the onset of cryptocurrencies, you could effectively run the mining algorithms on your computer as an individual miner. The regular computer at your home or office operates on a CPU or central processing unit which was powerful enough to handle mining functions.

Mining at the onset simply meant downloading or compiling the correct mining software and the wallet for a preferred coin. A miner would then configure the mining software to join their preferred cryptocurrency network then dedicate your computer to the task of mining cryptocurrencies.

In recent months and years, miners turned from CPU computers to GPU-based PCs. The GPU is the graphics processing unit that processes video systems on your computer. Basically, a GPU is like a CPU but a lot more powerful and designed to execute specific tasks. It is this specialization that makes the GPU suited for tasks such as cryptocurrency mining.

Compare CPU vs. GPU Capacity

A CPU core can execute only 4 or 32-bit instructions per clock while a GPU can execute 32—32-bit instructions in the same period of time. This simply means a GPU processor executes 800 times more instructions per clock.

Even though the latest, most modern CPUs have even 12 cores and much higher frequency clocks, still one GPU, like the HD5970, is more than 5 times faster than 4 modern CPUs combined. Therefore, GPU mining can result in faster transaction times and you can gain more coins in the same time frame.

Functions of the GPU versus the CPU

The CPU is the executive arm of the computer. The central processing unit is essentially a decision maker that is directed by the software in use. CPUs do all sorts of mathematical computations. On the other hand, a GPU is more of a laborer than an executive. GPUs contain large numbers of ALUs, or arithmetic and logic units. This makes them capable of executing large quantities of bulky mathematical labor in a greater quantity than CPUs.

What you need to be concerned with is the fact that the advent of GPU mining has made CPU mining almost obsolete. This is because the hash rate of most cryptocurrency networks increased exponentially. CPU mining is hardly profitable on some cryptocurrency networks but is thriving on others. It has largely been affected by the increased hash rate.

GPU mining is significantly faster in comparison and hence profitable on all cryptocurrency systems. Today, cryptocurrency mining heavily relies on GPU-based mining rigs. A mining rig is a computer system or arrangement that is used for mining coins. Most rigs are dedicated to accomplishing only one task, which in this case, is crypto mining.

Buying GPUs

When it comes to considering specific graphics cards for your mining rig, the first choice for many miners is the NVIDIA GeForce 1080 Ti which provides the greatest overall hashing power of any GPU on the market, though it is also known to consume more power when under a full mining load than any other GPU as well.

The more midrange option is currently the GTX 1070 or the AMD Radeon RX 480 for a more balanced mix of performance and power consumption. In fact, with the proper modifications, the GTX 1070 can generate performance that is nearly on par with the 1080 Ti while still consuming significantly less power overall.

While the popularity of cryptocurrency mining means that the market for GPUs is occasionally hit with artificial market scarcity as miners buy up the whole supply as soon as it is released, you should typically be able to find a GTX 1070 for under $500. When they are hard to find, however, you can easily see the price skyrocket to $700 or more. If you find that the prices you are seeing are in this upper range, then you will likely want to keep a close eye on Amazon for when a new shipment hits the market as you will then be more likely to find it at the traditional MSRP.

With the GTX 1070 in hand, you can then make use of a program known as MSI Afterburner to increase the memory interface clock to 650 MHz and reduce the power target to 66 percent to decrease heat output and board power consumption as much as possible. This, in turn, will ensure that GPU temperatures remain around a reasonable 66 degrees Celsius which is nearly 15 degrees cooler than what it would be running at without the tweaks. This, in turn, raises the average hash rate from 27.24 MH/s to 31.77 MH/s. With this hashing power, combined with an average power consumption of 177 and a cost per kilowatt hour at 10 cents, you are looking at a profit of about $140 per month.

Proof of Work vs. Proof of Stake

Proof of Work was designed as a protocol to achieve consensus and deter or prevent cyber attacks, especially distributed denial-of-service or DDoS. Such attacks have the sole purpose of diminishing or even exhausting the resources of computer systems through repeated sending of fake requests.

Proof of Work concept has been around for many years, way before cryptocurrencies. Today, it is adopted by different cryptocurrency systems such as Ethereum, Bitcoin, and Litecoin because it allows distributed consensus across systems. It is used mainly to create decentralized agreements about adding blocks to the network between different computers or nodes within the network.

HashCash is an example of Proof of Work function used by Bitcoin. Bitcoin miners spend a lot of time mining the currency. For a block to be added to the network, HashCash needs to produce very specific data that will verify the amount of work that goes into producing the currency.

Proof of Work is Integral to Crypto Mining

Being the traditional mining method many of the older cryptocurrencies use, Proof of Work has become an essential requirement when mining cryptocurrencies.   When cryptos are mined, miners verify transactions on blocks are legitimate. In order for the verification to happen, miners have to solve a complex mathematical problem. This problem is also known as the proof-of-work problem.

One thing to note is that as the network increases in size and the coins gain in value, the problems become increasingly harder to solve. Therefore more computational power is required as we move forward, I discuss this in greater depth in the chapter "Why I don't recommend you mine Bitcoin".

Proof of Stake

Another aspect that is commonplace with crypto mining is Proof of Stake. Proof of stake is another different method of validating crypto transactions. It is an algorithm that produces the same result as Proof of Work but using a different process. Proof of Stake came much later and was first used in 2012.

While Proof of Work algorithm compensates miners who solve mathematical problems, Proof of Stake identifies miners using a different approach. On the Proof of Stake protocol, there is no block reward. This is because digital currencies using this system are pre-mined and their number does not change. Since there is no block reward, miners are paid a transaction fee and are referred to as forgers instead.

Benefits of Proof of Stake over Proof of Work

- Validators do not have to use any computing power.

- It saves validators a lot of money in energy costs.

- Proof of Stake ensures a safer network.

- It makes attacks very costly because those doing the attacking must own a significant proportion of the coins themselves. Therefore they are essentially attacking their own coins. It would be like robbers deciding to rob a bank they owned 51% of.

Why I Don't Recommend You Mine Bitcoin

Whenever Bitcoin's price is rising (and that's most of the time!), the mining question always pops up. Usually from those who are inexperienced or want a "free" way to get a piece of the pie.

It all starts with a variant of this question.

"Why buy Bitcoin at $100/$1,000/$4,000 when you can just use your computer to mine some for free?"

Unfortunately, like everything else - there is no such thing as free Bitcoin.

As previously discussed, the way Bitcoins are created or "mined" is by using a computer to solve an of increasingly complex series of algorithms. Users are then rewarded for solving these algorithms by receiving Bitcoin. There is no man power involved, you yourself don't have to solve the algorithm, you just have to link your computer up to the Bitcoin network and the computer does the rest. There are also no shortcuts or breakthrough moments, the only way Bitcoin can be obtained quicker is with more computer power. How much computational power you supply determines the size of your reward. The more power you supply, the more Bitcoins you receive.

Now here is why mining is generally a terrible investment for the average Joe.

1. Electricity Costs - The electricity costs involved with running your computer 24/7 (which is necessary for mining) by far outweigh the amount of Bitcoins you receive for completing the task. You require access to industrial electricity rates of around $0.02 per kWh in order for the venture to be

profitable on a small scale. The vast majority of people cannot access these rates without some sort of special connection.

2. Requiring Specialist Hardware - Nowadays, the most efficient mining processes require special hardware known as Application-specific integrated circuits (ASIC). ASICs can be described as a supercomputer that can only ever perform one task. Specialist Bitcoin ASIC miners available for consumer purchase still start at around $1000 and often run around $2000-$2500.

3. Equipment maintenance - To maintain all this computing power is an additional cost. The cost of cooling alone is a large cost that has to be factored into long term profits. Hardware running 24/7 burns out faster and replacement mining equipment will be needed in due course.

4. The increasing size of the Bitcoin network - The network pays out a fixed amount of Bitcoin, regardless of how many miners are using the network. The current rate is around 1800BTC per day, which sounds like a huge number until you realize just how many miners there are on the network. The current mining power is equivalent to 17.6 BILLION desktop computers. Therefore the average payout for the end user running 1 desktop computer, with a standard, not designed for mining GPU, full time is approximately $0.000107 per day. Or roughly 2 cents a year's worth of BTC. To put it lightly, you have more chance of winning the lottery than you do making a profit from mining Bitcoin your standard home computer.

Mining in 2017 is a much different proposition from mining in 2010 or even 2012. There are some opportunities which involved investing in Bitcoin farms or group purchasing processing power of ASIC at a discount. This is known as a "mining pool". Due to cheaper power costs currently around 80% of the world's mining pools are based in China, with Iceland possessing the second largest number. Joining a mining pool requires a lower upfront investment but still requires cheap electricity rates and have debatable ROI potential.

It should also be worth noting that many of those who promote group mining or cloud mining do so under an affiliate program with whatever company that is promoting, meaning they get a commission % every time someone signs up.

However, for the average Joe without a huge amount of money to invest - I would strongly recommend buying coins instead of mining them. You are more likely to get higher returns in both the short and long run.

Ethereum Mining & Switch to Proof of Stake

Ethereum is one of the most popular cryptocurrencies on the market today and is second only to Bitcoin in terms of popularity and market capitalization. Ethereum mining is the process of mining Ether, the token used on this cryptocurrency system. Ether provides the only pathway of using this powerful network.

Ether mining does not just increase ether volumes but also helps secure the network. When ether is mined, it creates, verifies, propagates, and publishes blocks on the blockchain. We can conclude, therefore, that mining ether also secures the network and ensures transactions are verified.

There are major organizations and developers running smart contracts on Ethereum network. In fact, ether is looked at as an incentive to motivate developers who wish to create powerful applications.

Essentially, a developer has to mine ether which will be used on the network or sold to interested buyers later. Executing transactions on Ethereum network is a much cheaper method of using the network compared to buying ether directly.

How Ethereum Mining Works

Ethereum mining is very similar to Bitcoin mining. For each block of transactions, miners have to repeatedly compute and come up with a solution to a complex mathematical puzzle. In other words, Ethereum miners have to run a block's unique metadata through a hash function. The metadata includes software version and timestamp.

The hash then returns a scrambled, fixed length string of letters and numbers. Only the nonce value changes which in turn affects the resulting hash value. When a miner finds the hash that matches the current target, he or she will be rewarded with ether and the entire blockchain will be updated with this information.

If you are mining a particular block but another miner finds its hash, then you will have to cease work on that block and begin working on the next block. It is almost impossible for anyone to cheat at crypto mining. You cannot fake the work and then emerge with the correct solution to the puzzle. This is why they use Proof of Work protocol to secure the network. However, verifying transactions takes almost no time.

Miners find a block approximately every 12 to 15 seconds. Should this speed get faster or slow down, then the Ethereum algorithm will automatically reset the difficulty level of the mathematical puzzle. The readjustments of the difficulty level are meant to maintain the solution time at 12 – 15 seconds.

Mining profitability depends a lot on luck and the amount of computing power devoted to the mining process.

Ether mostly uses a Proof of Work algorithm known as Ethash. Ethash demands more memory so that it is difficult to mine using these costly ASIC computers which are specialized computers with advanced processors that are largely used to mine Bitcoin.   This is probably why there are no ASICs specifically designed for mining ether.

Even then, Ethereum mining will not go on forever.   The network is transitioning from Proof of Work to Proof of Stake. Proof of Work essentially protects the network from tampering and determines which transactions are valid. On the other hand, proof of stake is where stakeholders secure the network through their own tokens.

How to Start Mining Ethereum

The process of mining is considered as the glue that holds the entire Ethereum network together. It achieves this by engaging in consensus on any changes that take place on the applications running on the network.

As a miner, you need to add your computer to a node in the network to join others trying to solve complex mathematical puzzles. You need to try a large number of mathematical problems until one of them gets solved and releases new ether.

Joining the Network

In theory, anyone with a computer can join the Ethereum network and begin mining coins. However, as more and more miners join, the blockchain requires more and more power so that joining now requires a very powerful computer. To be successful, you will need a high-powered computer with the appropriate mining software.

Find Appropriate Mining Hardware

As you already know by now, to mine ether, you require specialized computer hardware that will be dedicated to full-time computer mining. Ideally, you can choose between CPU or GPU mining hardware.

However, as of today, CPUs have become almost a novelty and only GPU hardware is available, especially for Ethereum mining.

There are plenty of GPU computers in the market and setting up one is not a simple task. First find out which particular models are the most profitable based on parameters such as power consumption, hash rate performance and cost. It is advisable to set up a mining rig. A mining rig is simply a system of GPU computers assembled together. Such a rig might take you up to a week to set up.

You should work out your profitability, so you know how much profit you will be making. There are mining calculators available that can help you compute your expected profitability. The most accurate one right now can be found at CryptoCompare.com/mining

The results will let you know how much ether you will earn at a particular hash rate.

Ethereum's Switch from Proof of Work to Proof of Stake Protocols

Ethereum is expected to make its biggest upgrade ever. According to its inventor, Vitalik Buterin, Ethereum will move from use of Proof of Concept to Proof of Stake. The switch and adoption is expected to end in about one year's time.

Ethereum is expected to achieve this move by implementing the software known as Casper. Casper v1 is a hybrid of Proof of Work and Proof of Sale concepts. This software is going to decrease and finally end the use of Proof of Concept. This essentially means that Ethereum mining will no longer be profitable.

What is Casper?

Casper is a Proof of Stake algorithm that will start running on the Ethereum network this year (2018). The first version of the software is a hybrid of both Proof of Concept and Proof of Stake. However, it is expected that Proof of Concept consensus will eventually be eliminated so a lot of the power that miners currently have will be removed. Also, Proof of Stake algorithm uses far less energy to operate the network. It offers additional protection such as reduced centralization and preventing 51% attacks.

The Ethereum community believes that this switch will help address the problem of scalability that the network is currently facing. Casper will allow the network to scale more efficiently and also enable new blocks to be created faster and added to the network. Scalability will be managed through a process known as sharding. Sharding is the process of partitioning a large database horizontally into smaller and easily managed parts.

Benefits of Shift from PoW to PoS

The Network will not consume as much power as is currently the case. It is estimated that both Ethereum and Bitcoin consume $1 million worth of energy and hardware per day just to keep the networks up and running.

The network will not need to issue as many coins as it currently does in order to motivate participants to keep operating within the network. PoS will discourage the formation of centralized cartels that may cause harm to the network. The 51% attacks will be minimized as economic penalties can be used to make the attacks very costly.

Will Miners be Affected by this Shift?

The profitability of mining on the Ethereum network will definitely be affected. Miners will not earn as much as they currently do. The complete shift to PoS is expected to take between one and two years so there is no immediate effect on current miners.

The Ethereum community has agreed to this shift so it will happen. Starting 2018, the reward from a single block will decrease from 5 ether to 3 ether. Miners can start mining other coins such as Ethereum Classic or Monero.

To understand why this change could be so huge for Ethereum, it is important to understand just how it differs from the proof of work model. With a proof of stake verification system, instead of having the miner solve the equation in order to verify the block, a validator, who is confirmed reliable by the stake they have in the system, will commit to its accuracy, knowing that if they lie they will lose their own ether as well. The Alliance is currently testing the new system through a limited use verification process to make sure it is ready for a wider launch soon.

This will ultimately serve to make mining more egalitarian as a whole as it will no longer be based around who has the best mining machine, thus leveling the playing field as all the mining will be done on the blockchain itself. It will also serve to make 51 percent attacks more difficult to pull off as it requires direct contact with other miners as opposed to just having enough hardware to brute force the blockchain successfully.

Mining Versus Buying Cryptocurrencies

At this point, you're probably wondering if it is more profitable to buy coins than to mine them. Answering this question is not easy as there are many factors which affect the final outcome. However, it is possible to examine the two and come up with a reasonable conclusion. The question is if you had $10,000, would it be better to invest it in a mining operation or just buy coins?

Cloud Mining for Cryptocurrencies

Let us first try and understand different mining operations. Cloud mining has become rather popular in the recent past because it enables small investors to pool resources and participate in crypto mining. There are a number of companies that provide credible cloud mining services.

Cloud mining is a service that offers you an opportunity to invest a small amount of money and participate in the mining of a given cryptocurrency. What you are doing by joining such an operation is essentially to rent crypto mining hardware and receive a share of the mined coins in return.

As a participant in a cloud mining operation, you will be paying for a given hash rate for a set period of time. For instances, you can rent 10 THS for a 3-year period to mine Ethereum. Sometimes your contractual obligations may require that you pay for some expenses such as electricity and maintenance. These are often charged on a daily basis but billed weekly or monthly.

Pros and Cons of Cloud Mining

Pros

- As an investor, you do not need to invest in actual equipment. Crypto mining equipment can be quite expensive, especially high-end hardware.

- Setting up mining equipment can be tricky and time consuming. It can take up to one week just setting up a series of powerful crypto mining hardware. Fortunately, cloud mining members do not have to worry about equipment setup or even monitoring and maintenance.

- There is no need to worry about electricity things such as the noise and heat generated by the mining operation.

- You are also able to invest a relatively small amount of money in such a major operation and earn handsome returns. If done well, crypto mining can be a source of additional revenue and sometimes even your main source of income.

Cons

- As an investor in a cloud mining operation, you do not own any of the hardware or other equipment used in the operation. As such, you are left with no hardware at the end of your contract even though any money you paid upfront will not be returned.

- Sometimes it costs a lot more to join a cloud mining operation especially if you want a higher hash rate for a higher return on investment.

- You are not guaranteed that the cloud mining company will be there at the end of your contract. There is a certain level of risk involved here.

Crypto Buying versus Mining

To find out which one, between mining and buying, is more profitable, we need to find out how much we can make using either process by investing $10,000. At today's rate of 1BTC=$8,240 (as of Feb 7th, 2017), our $10,000 will fetch about 1.21 BTC. You can check the latest rates at sites such as www.CoinLlama.com.

Now we need to see if we can make more money than this through mining. It is never an easy thing working out profitability because of the many factors at play. Some of the variables involved include increasing mining difficulty and energy costs.

Find the Best Crypto Mining Equipment

Now since most of the $10,000 will be spent buying equipment, it is advisable to find the best in the market. The main issue you are likely to face is that most credible mining products are often out of stock and so you may have to create a pre-order. However, if you search harder, you are likely to find excellent products. You can check out companies like Butterfly Labs or Bit-Main.

Calculate the Number of Bitcoins You Can Mine with $10,000

You can easily find a Bitcoin mining calculator online which you can use for this purpose. Even then, there are some variables that still remain unknown and you will have to work with estimates. One of these variables is the rate at which the mining difficulty will increase while the other is the exchange rate of Bitcoin with time.

The equipment you need might cost something like $8000. This is the cost of about 7 Antminer S4-B2 miners. You do not have to host the computers at home or in your office. Instead, you can have them hosted in China where hosting and energy costs are quite low. These machines are also quite noisy and generate plenty of heat. The rest of the costs including shipping, daily hosting, and electricity amount to a little over 9,200. The balance can pay for electricity and hosting costs for a period of about three months. Daily expenses are roughly around $7.2.

Now, most calculators show that you are likely to make just about the same amount of crypto initially invested. This means that, in some instances, buying and mining coins add up to almost the same amount.

Ethereum Mining versus Buying

Ethereum mining seems to be a lot more profitable than buying. Take the example of tech researchers who invested 1500 Euros in a mining operation and another 1500 Euros buying ether. They mining rig was mining Ethereum at 147 MH/s. This was a real experiment that was conducted starting June 2016.

Outcomes

The 1500 Euros bought 136 ETH or ether tokens. However, after 6 months, the mining rig had generated almost 105 ETH. By the end of March 2016, the researchers had mined over 140 ETH. By June of 2017, the mining operation had earned about 152 ETH compared to the 136 initially purchased.

In both operations, it seems like mining has an edge over buying. This is true because you can continue mining coins for a long time, recover your initial investment, and continue making money.

The only downside is that machines do break down with time, hash rates change, and conditions in the crypto mining sector hardly remain the same. There are always policy changes and so on.

In conclusion, if you want to make instant money, then invest in cryptocurrencies, subject to performance in the market. However, for long term investment, then mining may well be the better of the two options.

Pros of Crypto Mining

- You can work out how much you will expect to earn on a weekly, daily, or monthly basis

- It provides an additional source of income

- Once you set up the mining rig, you can set it and forget it. It doesn't need constant monitoring or tinkering.

- You can continue mining for a long time to come

- You get to keep any equipment that you buy and then resell it if you decide to no longer mine yourself

Cons of Crypto Mining

- The equipment needed is very expensive

- Mining generates a lot of noise and heat

- The equipment can break down from time to time

- You have to learn how to set it up, which can be daunting for some.

- Crypto mining computers consume a huge amount of energy daily

Pros of Buying Crypto

- You can purchase cryptocurrencies at any time at market rates

- There is no need to invest in any equipment

- You receive your investment's worth instantly

- Transaction fees are negligible

Cons of Buying Crypto

- Price fluctuations may affect your investment

- Exchanges often charge buyers high fees

How to Setup your Own Mining Rig

Building your own cryptocurrency mining rig is more like growing your own money tree. You will create wealth in the form of cryptocurrencies even as you go about your daily business.

What is a mining rig? A mining rig refers to a system of computers that are set up together for purposes of mining cryptocurrencies such as Ethereum or Bitcoin. Mining is the process of extracting crypto tokens from a blockchain network.

A mining rig can be dedicated, which means it has been constructed and set up specifically to mine cryptocurrencies. The rig can also be a system of computers that have the capacity to mine crypto coins.

Setting up a Rig

Setting up a mining rig is a two-step process. First, you will have to identify the equipment that you need. Choosing and sourcing the right equipment for your preferred mining operation. The second step involves putting the equipment together. Putting the rig together is a technical process that is similar but more complex to building your own computer.

Mining rigs consist of similar components found in most desktop computers. However, there are a couple of differences. For instance, in your regular desktop computer, there is a general balance between components such as HD, GPU, RAM, and CPU. With mining rigs, you want a very basic HD, bare minimum RAM memory, the lowest clocked CPU and 5 – 7 GPUs. It is not possible to fit this kind of equipment in a normal computer case, so you will most likely need a custom-made case that will hold all your equipment.

How to Pick the Correct Mining Rig Parts

GPU Mining Cards

GPU stands for graphics processing units. When it comes to GPUs, you want to select the very best in the market. Basically, search for GPUs with low power usage, low cost, and a high hash rate. It's easier to start with just one GPU then scale up to 5 or 6. Anything beyond 7 will be difficult to stabilize. You should aim to find a balance between a GPU with low power consumption and the highest hash rate. The hash rate denotes the speed at which it can mine cryptocurrencies.   There is quite a variety of GPUs to choose from, depending on the currency that you intend to mine. Make sure you do not buy your GPUs or any other components off a street corner because they often have problems that you won't notice until you get home and plug in the card. However, you can find good quality, second hand processors at reputable outlets.

Mining Rig Case

As already noted above, crypto mining rigs cannot fit in regular computer cases. You will need to either buy a custom-made case or build your own. You can easily build your own case at home. Most miners do so using either plastic storage crates or a milk case. They both function really well even though they may not look that great. You can even choose to create a wooden case if you wish. It's really all up to you, aesthetics are not our main focus here.

Power Supply

The standard desktop computer uses a standard power supply ranging from 300W – 500W. When it comes to a mining rig, you will require a lot more power. If you create a mining rig with 6 to 7 GPUs, you need to ensure that you have access to sufficient power. You should have access to at least 1,200W. The supply efficiency should be certified at Gold or better. Make sure that the power supply is modular so that you configure your cables individually. This will turn out to be extremely important when building your rig.

A Motherboard

A motherboard is essential the brain of your computer and forms the base of your mining rig. It is on the motherboard that you build everything. When searching for one, you will be looking to find one with sufficient GPU slots because these will determine the number of GPUs or graphics card that can be accommodated. The number of GPUs will also determine, in the end, your total hash power. Most GPUs work on a PCI express so find a motherboard with at least 3 PCI Express slots. You can fit 3 GPUs on this motherboard each with a hash rate of 20 MH/s so that in total you have 60 MH/s. You can also opt for CPU-Motherboard combinations which are readily available. For purposes of coin mining, you will have to maximize the number of GPUs that your motherboard can support. Find one that can accommodate between 6 and 7 GPUs. Such motherboards are hard to find in stores, so you may want to search for them online. Great examples include the ASUS Prime Z270-P Motherboard or the Intel Celeron G3930.

Powered Riser Cables

Also crucial for your mining rig are powered riser cables. You will need these to extend PCI-e connections from the motherboard. This way, you will be able to mount the GPUs within your crate, or case. You should find as many PCI cables as you can and ensure that they match up with the total number of GPUs that you have.

Hard Drive

You will require a suitable hard drive where you will store your mining software and operating system. A good, solid state drive will do just fine. SSD hard drives are so called because they do not have any moving parts which can break or give in. the size will basically depend on what things you will do when mining so take that into consideration. For instance, if you need to download the entire blockchain, then you will need a sizeable hard drive to store the blockchain. However, if you have no such intentions, then a standard, 120 GB SSD will do.

The Operating System

Linux has some of the most powerful operating systems capable of mining multiple coins such as Monero, Z-cash, and Ethereum. There are also Window's based mining operating systems. Some are specific such as the Eth OS which is the operating system that mines Ethereum on Linux. There are a couple of others to choose from so ensure that you choose the correct one for whichever coin you are focusing on.

Accessories and Other Essential Components

You will also require additional components for your mining rig. These include RAM memory, a basic monitor and mouse, and a couple of box fans. Get a single fan for each separate rig. For the RAM, you will need a single 4GB 1600MHz and nothing more.

Put the Mining Rig Together

Now that you have all the components with you, you need to put it all together. If you have experience building a PC, then this will not be much different. You will probably find it easy. However, anyone can learn how to assemble a mining rig.

Crypto Wallet

First things first, you will need a cryptocurrency wallet. The wallet will store the coins you mine. You will want to get a reliable hardware wallet such as the Ledger Nano S. This wallet is immune to viral and malware attacks and just cannot be hacked.

The monitor will provide you with additional security because it displays crucial wallet details. You can use the Ledger Nano S to store Bitcoins, Litecoin, Z-cash, Dash, DodgeCoin, and Ethereum.

How to Put it All Together

First, confirm that your power supply unit is able to handle the GPU cards in your system. Also, ensure that your riser cables can reach your additional GPUs within your rig. The GPUs should be safely located and secured. So, set up the GPUs and ensure they are well distributed. Remember that GPUs do get quite hot and they generate plenty of heat. Place the GPUs in a well-ventilated room. Also, ensure that your rig is mining once it is set up.

First install the operating system, followed by the mining software onto your PC. You can choose either Ubuntu from Linux or Windows from Microsoft. Windows is preferable because it has automated the installation of drivers. This enables all components within your computer to communicate and interact easily. However, Ubuntu is free and offers you more options.

Once the GPUs have been set up and attached to the motherboard, you will need to check that everything else is in place. For instance, are the fans available to cool the GPUs? Once everything is setup, you can test the equipment and then proceed to mine your preferred cryptocurrency. If you want to mine Ethereum, then you can download EthOs. This is an APP specifically designed for mining Ethereum. While it is advisable to have this APP, it is not essential and you can do without it.

Beginning Mining

Now that your equipment is all set up, you can then begin the mining process. There are two different approaches that you can use. These are solo mining and pool mining.

Solo mining: As a solo miner, you will be working against the other miners because you will be competing to mine ether. If you rig is able to generate the correct hash, then you earn the block reward. If you have a rig of 60 MH/s against the network's 1.2 GH, you will not earn ether as often as you would want. You may also have to download the entire blockchain. You will need sufficient memory space for this.

Pool mining: This is a crypto mining process where you join other miners and team up in order to minimize the volatility of your earnings. This way, you will be able to earn ether every day due to increased hash power. The reward you get on a regular basis will be equivalent to the amount of work your system puts in. You will also not have to download the entire blockchain onto your computer.

You can choose to join programs such as Miner Gate for more efficient pool mining. Miner Gate allows its members to mine coins via options. You can also mine two different currencies at the same time and without losing any hash rate that is geared towards your main currency. However, Miner Gate is not the only option you have, and you can still join other less sophisticated mining pools.

Equipment Cost

Mining equipment is not cheap especially the latest models which are specifically designed for crypto mining. It should be noted, all these ROI figures are just an estimate based on the prices at the time of writing. Actual returns figures will vary.

L3+ Antminer ASIC: This mining equipment costs about $1580 on average. It has a hash rate of 504 MH/s and can bring in a return of about $5.15 per day. You can expect a payback on your investment in 305 days.

Bitmain Antminer S9: One of the best pieces of mining equipment is the Antminer S9. It is designed to mine Bitcoin and is a very costly piece of equipment. It costs $6,600 at Amazon and has an impressive hash rate of 14 TH/s.

Bitmain Antminer S7: The Antminer S7 from Bitmain costs $1,400. It comes with a hard disk of 512 MB, SD-RAM memory and operates on a Linux platform.

Antminer Power Supply: The power supply for the Antminer costs $170. Second hand versions are much cheaper, costing about $130.

What is Cloud Mining?

Cloud mining can be described as the process of mining cryptos via a remote data center where mining power is shared among members. Such arrangements enable interested members to join the cloud and participate in coin mining operations without the need to buy or manage the hardware.

In cloud mining operations, mining rigs are located and maintained within a facility owned or rented by a mining company. Members simply need to register and purchase shares or mining contracts in return for a share of the mining rewards. However, there are weekly or monthly costs such as overheads, rent, and electricity costs that have to be paid. This amount is normally deducted from the earnings of the cloud members.

Therefore, if you want to invest in coin mining operations without the trouble of buying and managing your own hardware, there is an alternative in cloud mining. By joining a could mining operation, you get to share processing power with other remote miners. All you need to join a cloud is your own computer for communication purposes, a wallet to receive your pay and payment required for sign up.

Different Types of Hosting

Companies providing cloud mining services can either lease a virtual private server or a physical mining server then install mining software. Sometimes these companies opt for hashing power hosted at a data center instead of leasing dedicated servers. Hashing power is normally denominated in GH/s or GigaHash per second. The contracts signed often indicate the period for the contract and desired hashing power.

Pros of Cloud Mining

- Mining operations are outside your premises. This means a quiet, cool home.

- No additional energy costs.

- You will not be stuck with costly equipment should miner stop being profitable.

- You will not experience any ventilation problem.

- There is very little chance of being let down by equipment suppliers.

The Cons of Cloud Mining

Cloud mining can sometimes be a risky option. Some of these risks are described below;

- Mining operations are opaque in nature and lack transparency.

- There is a risk of fraud.

- Reduced earnings as profits are split and costs have to be paid.

- There is a general lack of control and flexibility.

Avoiding Cloud Mining Scams

Investments in cryptocurrencies have grown immensely in the last one year. Plenty of small term investors earn a recurring income through cloud mining. Here are a couple of things to watch out for.

1. Must have ASIC Miner vendor support: Ideally, any legit miner will voluntarily and willingly let you know about their provider and IT support firm they are dealing with. If a company does not have such support, then it probably is suspicious.

2. Data Center and mining equipment photos: A genuine cloud mining operation should have photos of its data center and mining equipment on its website. Any firm that cannot show you photos of its operations is honestly not worth investing in. Some companies even show proof of electricity bills, so you should not take any excuses from companies that do not provide photos.

3. Check for presence of mining address: Any legitimate cloud mining company is likely to display its public mining address. Many of the legitimate ones actually do, like Genesis Mining. If the firm is unable to provide one, then it most likely is not genuine.

4. Take a look at the company's registration: Genuine cloud mining companies often have every clear registration with proper domains and are open. They should never be anonymous as they are supposed to be very open with members or investors. Full contact details, for instance, are absolutely essential. When these are missing, such as an official address, phone number, and so on, then it is probably a scam so avoid such a firm.

5. Watch out for referrals: Cloud mining sector makes thin profits because there are many members who have to be paid as well as certain costs such as electricity, rentals and so on. As such, they cannot afford to have referral programs that pay 5% or 10%. Any cloud mining firm offering to pay such high fees to affiliates is probably not genuine so take your money and run.

6. Be cautious when they offer guaranteed profits: In cloud mining operations, profits or income are never guaranteed. However, a scammer will try all ways and means to lure you into their scam. Also, some companies provide no option to withdraw your earnings. This is actually absurd. You should be allowed to withdraw your earnings whenever you want. Firms with opaque payment systems and those with unclear withdrawal processes should be avoided like the plaque. Please keep off such websites to avoid losing your money.

Basically, there are plenty of red lights to watch out for. You need to be comfortable with a company's profile and image. If you have any doubts or feel like something just does not add up, then your instincts are probably right. Make sure you find only genuine companies, check the reputation and reviews online and if you feel confident enough, you are probably right.

Guaranteed Returns in Cloud Mining Operations

If you join a cloud mining firm, you will enjoy certain benefits. While you are likely to get a return on investment in a couple of months, it is not possible to give a certain guarantee of return on investment. The reason is that cryptocurrency mining relies on a couple of factors, one of these being luck with regards to market prices for your chosen coin.

Since luck is a factor in mining, getting a return on investment is not always guaranteed. It is possible to earn a good return every day over a long period of time. It is also possible to finally recover your initial investment. However, no cloud company should give you a guaranteed return as it is not in control of the entire process. If you join a reputable crypto mining company, then you are likely to make your money back and keep earning a residual income for some time. Not all companies are able to provide you with the kind of return you would want.

List of Noted   Mining Scams to Avoid

There are a number of cloud mining programs that are Ponzi schemes masquerading as legitimate mining operations, or have already been proven to be Ponzi schemes. Many of since shut down, but unfortunately, some are still running to this day. Below is a list of some of the schemes you can avoid.

1hashmining.com - Ponzi scheme pretending to be a mining operation. Update: The website has now been shut down by authorities

50BTC.com - A mining pool that stopped paying out. The host's whereabouts are currently unknown.

7cly.com - A mining scam that promises returns of 2% per day. You should know by now that this just isn't realistic in any market.

Minerjet.com - Another one with guaranteed returns promised. Stay well away.

Mininghub.io - Another cloud mining operation. This one has a made up UK limited company behind it. Avoid like the plague.

Store4mining.com - A website claiming to sell mining hardware. They don't, only use trusted sources to purchase mining equipment.

Bc-prime.com - This one was actually running Google Ads for a while so even the world's biggest search engine thought they were legit. Fake mining platform which will steal your cryptocurrency.

Bitcoin-mining.group - This and all subdomains (which are focused on other coins like XRP) are fraudulent.

Bitminer.world - This one makes you send in more Bitcoin if you want to withdraw your earnings. Absolute sham high yield Ponzi scheme, and an utter disgrace to the mining world.

An Introduction to Mobile Mining

It is possible to mine cryptocurrencies using your mobile phone. There are apps in the market available for android smartphones that can mine cryptocurrencies. However, it is a challenging prospect as mining operations require a lot of power and consume huge quantities of energy.

Bitcoin and Ethereum mining operations require mining rigs. They consume huge quantities of energy, so such operations can hardly be performed on your smartphone. The only possibility of mining these major coins is to get one of the latest and most powerful smartphones in the industry then connect it to a mining pool. Therefore, mining the way we know it using a mining rig is not possible via smartphones.

Mobile Mining Apps

There are certain apps that you can download that will mine cryptos for you. These are mostly android apps so if you have a powerful smartphone, think about downloading one of these apps and begin mining immediately.

1. DroidMiner BTC/LTC Miner: This is a bitcoin mining app that lets you mine cryptocurrencies if you connect to a pool. It connects to the Get-Work pool. It is only through the pooling of resources that smartphones can actually mine altcoins such as Ethereum. Droid Miner is an Android based tool that was developed by ThatGuy. The architecture of the DroidMiner is based on Pooler's CPuminer and AndLTC Miner software.

Apart from Bitcoin, you can also mine Litecoin and Dodger Coin. In fact, it can mine all coins that use SHA-256 or scrypt. There are currently just under 500 users mining with this app and they give it an average rating of 3.5 out of 5.

2. Easy Miner: The Easy Miner is yet another pool mining application program. This app is easy to use, comes with an improved user interface, and displays crypto charts showing the latest prices. It also displays the network's hashing rates, so you are always aware of the mining situation.

3. LTC Miner: This is yet another android app that can be used to mine cryptocurrencies. It is specifically designed to mine within the Litecoin pool. You can easily join the pool and earn Litecoins on a regular basis.

While these apps are great for pool mining, they are still not suitable for actual mining using your phone's hardware mining just yet. Not until android develops much faster hardware will you be able to profitably mine on your phone.

MinerGate Mobile Miner

MinerGate is a mobile mining app for android phones. With this app, you can turn your smartphone into a portable mining rig. This was developed by an ordinary crypto miner who submitted it for a contest. It was such an impressive app that it was immediately adapted for use.

You first need to download the app onto your smartphone and then set it up. Once it is set up and ready to use, simply open an account with your details then log in. Now all you need to next is choose your preferred cryptocurrency. Simply find the coin you want to start mining and click on it.

Once you identify your preferred currency, simply start mining and earning. Ensure that you have a mobile wallet attached so that your earnings are storied in there. You can always check the balance any time you want. You can also see which currencies you are currently mining because, apparently, you can mine more than just one crypto.

Even as you mine, you are given plenty of options. For instance, you can choose to mine only when your smartphone is charging, or request mining to stop when the battery is low. You can choose to mine on the go so that you connect to the pool and mine coins as you go about your day.

Top Crypto-Mining Apps for Android

People all over the world are mining cryptos on their phones. They are mining Dogecoin, Bitcoin, Litecoin, and Ethereum among many others. If you want to start mining coins on your smartphone, then you can consider one of these apps. They are considered among the top android apps for coin mining.

1. BTC Safari
2. Bitcoin Farm
3. Easy Miner

However, before choosing an app to use, it is advisable to do your due diligence, learn more about the app before investing in one. Like previously stated, Bitcoin mining is not as profitable on your cellphone, so I'd recommend against any Bitcoin mining apps. You are better off mining smaller altcoins on your smartphone rather than Bitcoin.

How to Make Money Staking Coins

You can earn cryptocurrencies through a process known as staking. Many cryptocurrency investors are now looking at alternative investment streams and staking is certainly one of them.

What is staking? Staking is also referred to as Proof of Stake.

Proof of Stake is a concept where you buy coins and store them in your wallet for a given period of time, say, three months. It compares well with putting money in a fixed deposit account. You can save money in a fixed deposit account for a couple of months or weeks and then earn a decent return at the expiry of the said period.

Basically, Proof of Stake has so many technical benefits to any network. However, apart from these, investors also enjoy some economic benefits. They get to earn dividends by staking their coins in a particular wallet. Essentially you can make money by simply holding many POS (Proof of Stake) coins in the right wallet. This wallet is referred to as the staking wallet.

The system appreciates PoS because it helps secure the network and keep it stable. It also creates additional opportunities for network users to earn dividends based on their coins.

Understanding Basic Staking Terms

Distributed consensus: The term distributed consensus refers to a large group of investors who live in vastly different regions of the world but have a unifying agreement. In the world of cryptocurrencies, the agreement is mostly on the blocks or transactions that are valid and should be added to the network.

Proof of Stake: This is a specific algorithm that is used by some cryptocurrencies to manage their distributed consensus. It compares to Proof of Work and is considered a better alternative for achieving the same consensus.

Most Profitable Proof of Stake Cryptocurrencies

1. DASH: This cryptocurrency is also known as digital cash and is a very popular coin. It is among the first to introduce Proof of Stake and is built on Bitcoin's core but with better security and added privacy features. Dash does have a higher barrier to entry at 300 DASH to run a masternode, which gives 7.5% annual interest.

2. OKCash: This is yet another cryptocurrency that makes use of Proof of Stake. All you need to do is buy some of this currency and store in a stake-able wallet. OKCash currently has a 10% annual return for staking, with no minimum amount required, which makes it advantageous when compared to Dash for example.

3. NAV Coin: NAV Coin is among the first cryptocurrencies to operate on a dual blockchain. It's been in operation since 2014 and uses Proof of Stake for block verification and stability. You can use POS stake rewarding on this coin to earn extra cash regularly. This also enables you to earn even as you sleep, with an annual return rate of around 5%.

4. ReddCoin: ReddCoin is very popular on social media networks. You can use this POS based cryptocurrency to leverage content on social media to get handsome returns.

5. Stratis: This is another POS coin that you can use to stake and earn rewards. STRAT is the token that operates on the Stratis platform. You will, therefore, need a Stratis wallet to stake your tokens. While profits are not quite as high as with other coins, with time, this is expected to get better.

6. Neo: My personal favourite staking opportunity. Neo is similar to Ethereum in that it uses what is known as Gas (similar to Ether) to keep the network running. Unlike other Proof of Stake currencies, Neo doesn't require you to keep your wallet open at all times for staking.

Currently you require around 20 Neo to return 1 Gas, which represents an annual dividend of just less than 6%. The bonus with Neo is that as more applications run on the Neo network, the more Gas is needed, and thus your Gas is worth more. So you actually get a 1-2 punch of higher Neo values plus higher Gas values. This is what makes Neo my personal favourite of the staking coins.

Examples of Initial Investment vs. Expected Return on Investment

Remember that Proof of Stake operates in an almost similar manner to fixed deposit accounts. For fixed deposit accounts, you are paid an interest after maturity of the deposit. However, for Proof of Stake, the rewards you receive are crypto tokens.

1. The longer your coins are held in the staking wallet, the higher the rate of return. For instance, you receive 20% return after 3 months, 50% after 6 months, and 100% after a year. Thus the rate of return will depend on the maturity period.

2. The rate of return is sometimes calculated as simple or compounded interest.

Let us say you invest 100 ETH in a staking wallet for 3 months. At the end of 3 months, you will expect to earn 20% more ETH. This means you will own 120 ETH in that period of time.

*(100 * 20/100) + 100 = 120 ETH*

Please note that you can only stake with altcoins and not Bitcoin. Bitcoin rewards miners through the algorithm known as Proof of Work.

Advantages of Staking Crypto

The benefit of staking crypto is that you will not need to invest in expensive mining equipment. All you need to do is buy the coins you need then save them in a staking wallet. Then just sit back and watch your investment grow. It is a pretty decent, safe, and lucrative way to make money.

Another advantage of staking is that you get to have a predictable, secure, and guaranteed income. This is because the value of the coin increases predictably and its value at maturity can easily be determined. Staking does guarantee you will get your investment back.

Mining based stocks - An often overlooked opportunity

What if you could profit from cryptocurrency mining, without having to mine yourself? It's true, it's completely possible.

Two of the biggest cryptocurrency winners in the past few years, haven't been cryptocurrencies themselves, but ones that are affected by the boom in cryptocurrency mining.

You see, mining cryptocurrency requires a huge amount of computing power, in the form of Central Processing Units (CPUs) and Graphics Processing Units (GPUs). Manufacturers of these parts have seen their stock prices skyrocket since the beginning of 2016 when cryptocurrency mining really took off.

AMD ($AMD) and NVIDIA ($NVDA) are the two biggest winners thus far, in fact, in Q3 2017, NVIDIA's revenue from mining soared to $220 million for the quarter. Now, nearly 5% of the company's bottom line is attributable to cryptocurrency mining. AMD, on the other hand, sees roughly 10% of its overall revenue being from cryptocurrency mining sources.

The companies themselves have different approaches to how cryptocurrencies will affect their profits going forward. AMD CEO Lisa Su stated that they were expecting a "cryptocurrency cooling off period" in 2018, and the company doesn't consider demand for GPUs as a part of its long term gameplan.

NVIDIA, on the other hand, is more bullish and has openly admitted that it considers cryptocurrency mining a big part of future business plans.

So if you're into traditional investing as well as cryptocurrencies, it may be well worth checking out both of these stocks and seeing if they have a place in your portfolio.

Another Cryptocurrency Lending Scheme to Be Wary Of

In my previous books I have warned readers about BitConnect and DavorCoin, both of which are lending platforms that promised users guaranteed returns on investment. Like the regular financial world, you should be extremely skeptical of any platform that promises guaranteed returns. Since those books were published, both of these platforms have performed exit scams and taken thousands of dollars (millions in the case of BitConnect) from users. BitConnect and those who promoted it is currently in the process of a lawsuit for fraudulently acquiring assets. The same fate may well happen to DavorCoin.

In the meantime, however, there is a third lending platform that has been making waves recently in the shape of FalconCoin. According to their website, users will receive daily interest on coins with the monthly interest rate being 46%. That figure alone should have your alarm bells ringing because 46% interest in a month is a frankly absurd figure. The other big red flag is that investments must be locked up within the platform for a minimum of 180 days before users can withdraw them. They also claim you'll be able to "earn 180% by staking Falcon Coins".

Like these other lending platforms, FalconCoin, of course, has a referral program and is aiming to use social media to spread the word. This is what caused BitConnect to get extremely popular as larger YouTube channels (such as CryptoNick and Craig Grant who are both named in the BitConnect lawsuit) were advertising the project to their followers, who would sign up under their referral links. Referral programs don't necessarily mean a project is bad, however, if that ends up being the main source of income, as we see with many MLM/pyramid schemes, then we indeed have a problem. Through a few minutes of research, I already found multiple YouTube channels that were promoting FalconCoin and encouraging their viewers to sign up under their particular referral code.

Overall, FalconCoin displays the exact same red flags as BitConnect and DavorCoin before. Guaranteed returns and promises of ridiculously high interest rates are just too big to ignore, and as such, I would advise anyone to stay well away from the project.

Conclusion

Thank you for reading, and I hope what you read was informative and able to provide you with all of the tools you need to achieve your cryptocurrency mining goals, whatever they may be.

I encourage you to do additional research on top of what you've read here. Especially with regards to mining specific cryptocurrencies, as the procedure will be different for each one.

The next step is to find the best website where you can apply all the wonderful knowledge obtained through this book. Mining cryptocurrencies is a lucrative way of earning an extra stream of income, and many people just like you are making a decent secondary income from doing so. While this might not be your golden ticket to early retirement, who can say no to an extra few thousand dollars a year?

Remember, stay away from mining and lending platform scams. And with any investment you do make, only invest what you can afford to lose.

Thanks,

Stephen

Cryptocurrency: FAQ - Answering 53 of Your Burning Questions about Bitcoin, Investing, Scams, ICOs and Trading

Introduction

Hi,

For those of you already familiar with my books, the format of this one will be a little different. I won't be doing any in depth analysis of any particular coin. Nor will I be discussing any trading or investment strategies to employ.

Instead, I decided to do a question and answer format for questions I received from my email list, as well as some popular ones I found online that seemed to be asked over and over again. Some of these will be low level beginner questions, and I've decided to cover those first so the more experienced cryptocurrency investors can skip over them and move on to the more advanced section.

These questions were wide ranging and included topics like "Does coin X have greater potential than coin Y", as well as questions about government regulation, potential institutional adoption, the future of ICOs and much, much more.

I'd like to thank everyone who submitted a question, and I hope my answers cleared up any queries that you had.

So let's get to it.

Thanks,

Stephen Satoshi

Bitcoin

What's the easiest way to buy Bitcoin?

We'll get the most basic one out of the way. The best way for a completely new investor to invest in Bitcoin is to use Coinbase.

At one time, the most downloaded app on the App store, Coinbase allows users to buy, sell and store cryptocurrency. Coinbase is undoubtedly the most beginner friendly exchange for anyone looking to get involved in the cryptocurrency market. They currently allow trading of Bitcoin, as well as, Ethereum and LiteCoin using fiat currency as a base. As of January 1st 2018, you can now buy Bitcoin Cash on Coinbase as well. Known for their stellar security procedures and insurance policies regarding stored currency. The exchange also has a fully functioning iPhone and Android app for buying and selling on the go, very useful if you are looking to trade.

Once you are signed up and complete the identity verification procedures you can buy Bitcoin with your credit or debit card instantly.

Coinbase also recently launched the Coinbase Vault, which is a secure way of storing your cryptocurrency while still having it accessible to trade. The vault uses double email address + phone verification in order to access your funds. If you're planning on holding long-term, I still recommend offline storage - but as an intermediary option, the Vault is a step in the right direction.

If you sign up for Coinbase using this link, you will receive $10 worth of free Bitcoin after your first purchase of more than $100 worth of cryptocurrency.

http://bit.ly/10dollarbtc

Note, if you're going to be trading Bitcoin, I recommend doing so on Coinbase's partner platform GDax, which has lower fees.

I'm new to cryptocurrency how can I get started?

My personal recommendation would be to check out my Cryptocurrency: Beginners Bible book. It explains all the basic concepts behind cryptocurrency and blockchain technology and offers a primer to Bitcoin as well as 12 other of the more well known coins including Ethereum, Litecoin and Neo. There's also information about safely storing your coins.

How much Bitcoin does the Mt. Gox Trustee have? Could he dump it all at once? If he does will it cause a crash?

One of the more recent negative cryptocurrency stores came out in early March of 2018. For those of you who haven't been in the space for long, I'll catch you up on exactly what Mt. Gox is.

Mt. Gox was, at one time, the biggest cryptocurrency exchange in the world. At its peak, the Japanese exchange was handling over 70% of all Bitcoin transactions worldwide, which is a far higher number than any exchanges today.

The exchange was hacked in June 2013, which resulted in 850,000 Bitcoin being stolen by hackers. Roughly 5% of the total world supply of Bitcoin. This led to Mt. Gox filing for bankruptcy in February 2014 and CEO Mark Karpeles was arrested and charged with fraud and embezzlement by Japanese authorities.

Now, Mt. Gox was back in the news in 2018 when the bankruptcy trustee, sold over 18,000 Bitcoin (worth approximately $180 million) in one day, in order to pay creditors from the bankruptcy filing. Now, the trustee still holds over 166,000 Bitcoin, which if sold on the open market could cause massive downward pressure on price. Now, there has been a lot of speculation that the trustee is not allowed to sell more than a certain amount of Bitcoin per quarter, in order to keep the market somewhat stable. So it is doubtful that a huge sell off would occur any time soon, however, even selling as much as 10% of the holdings in one day would be concerning. Any further sales would also require approval from the bankruptcy court.

Many commentators have asked why the trustee didn't sell the Bitcoin at auction, like other bankruptcy assets are often sold, or why they didn't sell at an OTC desk like the FBI did with their seized Bitcoin from the Silk Road case. Either way, it is worrying that so much Bitcoin is in the hands of one person, whose sole goal is to extract as much fiat currency as possible from it.

Is it too late to buy Bitcoin?

It depends on exactly how you define "too late". If you're looking for 10000% gains in under 5 years then yes, it probably is too late. Some investors believe Bitcoin will eventually rise above $100,000 per coin, and a couple of more optimistic people have already put public statements out that they expect Bitcoin to reach $1 million per coin in the long run. Obviously these estimates are on the very bullish side, but the optimism is still there.

Where I believe Bitcoin can really shine is as a digital store of value - a "digital gold" if you will. It has already shown itself to be uncorrelated to the stock market, so could be a useful hedge against uncertain financial times during a market crash. The big factor in determining if Bitcoin can ever really reach this status is if volatility decreases as we move forward. Investment Banks have previously been reluctant to recommend such a volatile asset to their clients, and although we are seeing institutional adoption increase - this volatility will hamper further adoption.

Regardless of this, I believe Bitcoin has a place in all cryptocurrency portfolios because of its market leader position and influence on the price of other cryptocurrencies.

Can Bitcoin make banks disappear?

I think there's some level of confusion on this topic, which is why it deserves an answer here. In the original whitepaper, the "vision" for Bitcoin was as a trustless, peer to peer method of monetary transaction, which didn't require a third party (such as a bank), to verify said transactions, as the blockchain would do this.

The key thing to note with Bitcoin is that you yourself are your own bank. If you hold your private keys, the codes needed to actually spend your coins, then no one else has access to this, including a bank.

The real question emerges when we take into account Bitcoin's limited supply and deflationary nature. If people view Bitcoin as a method for day to day transactions, then we could see it eat into the market shares of banks. But if instead its position in cryptocurrency is indeed as a store of value, or "digital gold", then this is unlikely to affect banks going forward.

Other coins though may well do this. For example, if we see a scenario where Litecoin or Nano becomes the defacto day to day currency for people, and Bitcoin is looked at as a long term hedging asset. Then banks could well be in trouble.

In terms of making banks obsolete, this is unlikely in the near term at least. Banks will still be present as a service provider for insurance, personal loans, mortgages and such. Many banks are already developing their own blockchain solutions, and while this hasn't led to bank created coins yet, I wouldn't rule out the possibility that we will see some private bank-owned cryptocurrency experiments within the next 5 years.

Can you buy a fraction of a Bitcoin?

This is a big question from new investors in the cryptocurrency space, especially those who have only ever invested in stocks before. It may seem daunting when you see Bitcoin prices at $6,000, $9,000 or even $19,000 when the amount you wanted to invest was much smaller.

Fortunately, you can buy just a fraction of a Bitcoin. In fact, you can buy amounts as small as 0.0000001 Bitcoin. So even if you only want to test the waters with a small amount, this is entirely possible. All you have to do is set the dollar amount you want to invest in the Coinbase app or on the website and it will show you the fraction of Bitcoin you will receive in return.

Will the price of Bitcoin increase forever?

This is an interesting question, posed by a forum user. Due to the limited and fixed supply of Bitcoin (21 million), it is designed to be deflationary. In other words, it's value should theoretically increase indefinitely. Just like fiat currency's value would decrease indefinitely as more money is printed by central banks.

We won't truly know the answer to this question until all 21 million Bitcoin are in circulation, which is not scheduled to be until 2140, if the current mining difficulties do not change.

That, of course, does not take into account government regulation which could significantly affect the price one way or another. This is part of the reason why cryptocurrency as a whole is so volatile.

Then there is the big "what if" question regarding cryptocurrency becoming defacto day to day currency. For example, if the price of goods and services is measured in Bitcoin rather than fiat currency, then its primary use is no longer as a store of value, but as a regular currency. Therefore people will be encouraged to spend their Bitcoin, and the deflationary nature would pose problems.

Will the price of Bitcoin keep dropping?

This question relates to the early 2018 correction in which Bitcoin lost roughly 60% of its value in just 2 months. This will be alarming to all the new investors in the space, however, for those of us who have been around a while - it's nothing new.

In 2011, Bitcoin lost 94% of its value. Then in 2014, it lost 86% of its value. In 2017 alone we saw dips of 30% over 5 times, and yet these dips were then followed by even higher highs.

This is an all too familiar pattern in the Bitcoin world. Yet this time it has been receiving more media attention than before. For a medium term view, technical analysis shows there are support levels (people waiting to buy) for Bitcoin at $7.2K, $6K and $4.8K. If these levels are breached then I would start to worry as the support levels below them aren't as clear. However if these levels can hold, in other words, if more sellers don't emerge, then we will likely see an upswing again.

The big rises will come when we see increased adoption levels from Wall Street and institutional money coming in. Otherwise we could potentially be in for a full year of sideward movement like we saw in 2015.

When is the best time to buy Bitcoin?

The best time to buy Bitcoin was in 2010, the second best time is today. Cryptocurrency is far too volatile to try and time the market, so unless you are an experienced investor with a good grasp of technical analysis - your best option is to simply buy and hold.

You will need to get used to large upswings and downswings in price. For example, those who bought at the very top in late December are down roughly 60% at the time of writing. But those who bought 1 year ago are up roughly 500%. So once again, time in the market beats timing the market. So if you only invest what you can afford to lose, and can hold steady through the bad times, then you can receive large gains in the long run.

Cryptocurrency Investing

Why is the market so volatile?

A great question, and one all new investors in the space are wanting to know. There are a number of reasons for this and I'll explain them one by one.

The first is that this is the first asset ever to be born in the internet age. An age of instant gratification, an age of being able to do everything at the click of a button. Although online brokerage accounts for stocks have been around for some time now, the market as a whole was born in an age of stock tickers, and slow information. Cryptocurrency is the only market that is online 24/7 365, and thus, traders are always moving prices one way or another. Cryptocurrency trading is also a lot cheaper than trading other financial instruments, Binance, for example, takes 0.1% from all trades, whereas stock trading can be much more costly in terms of transaction fees.

The second one is the size of the market. Even at its peak of $800 billion in January 2018, that's still tiny compared to other financial markets. The global market cap for stock, for example, is around $80 trillion. Thus, it only takes a small amount of new money to move the market one way or another, especially if that money is institutional. $10 billion may seem like an enormous amount to you or I - but it's a drop in the ocean for large banks and hedge funds. This kind of money has the potential for huge effect on price one way or another.

The third is that because we are still in the early adoption stages of the market, any news, be it good or bad, tends to have a significant repercussion. For example, we saw a rumor of Ethereum founder, Vitalik Buterin's death cause the market to crash by 20%. Then we saw a fake news piece of "China bans cryptocurrency" cause another significant crash. In turn, 10 or 15% spikes in a day are the result of a US congressman speaking positively of cryptocurrencies.

These are the three big factors which contribute to volatility, and ones you should always be aware of, especially if you plan on trading frequently. For those of you planning to buy and hold, it will prepare you for days where we see red lines everywhere - but don't worry, these don't tend to last for long.

How many different coins should I own?

That is entirely up to you. As stated in previous books, I have always recommended having the majority of your portfolio in Bitcoin and Ethereum if you plan on investing for the long term. However, these are less likely to produce the 1000% gains we've seen in the past as they are now more mature assets than the rest of the cryptocurrencies.

In terms of other cryptocurrencies projects, I encourage you to do your own research on coins, and not blindly invest because of some hyped up marketing language on their website.

Another thing to remember is that the price of a coin is not an indicator of its potential growth. Market cap is a far more important indicator. For example, I see many new investors look at the price of Ripple and think "wow it could rise to $100 and I'll be rich". Ripple has the third biggest market cap right now at the time of writing ($27 billion), roughly one fifth of Bitcoin's market cap. Therefore at $100 per XRP, it would have a market cap of $3.9 trillion, which is 10X the total cryptocurrency market cap right now and just isn't realistic in this lifetime.

Generally speaking, coins with a market cap below $100 million can be considered smaller projects, with those below $20 million being looked at as microcap high risk projects.

How often should I take profits?

Everyone's financial situation is different, so I can't make any blind recommendations or a set period of time when you should take profits.

I still always recommend intermittently taking gains for yourself, and if you initial investments rise enough, you can be in a position where you cash out your initial investment and simply play with house money so to speak. This is probably the best position you can be in.

Will there ever be a chance to make 10000% returns again - or has that ship sailed?

We have to remember that we are still very much in the infant stages of cryptocurrency and blockchain technology. There is still only a small amount of money that has come in from Wall Street and other big institutional funds.

One thing to note is that the current value of the cryptocurrency market is roughly equivalent to what the Nasdaq value in the late 1980s, so we are still WELL before the Dotcom boom if you want something to compare it to.

There will be many projects that absolutely explode in the next few years. What those projects will be is another question entirely.

What evidence is there that institutional money really is coming in to the space?

Not all institutional investors take the same line as Warren Buffett or Charlie Munger. Even if the soundbites coming out are on the negative side, we must remember that these large investment banks and hedge funds are spending hundreds of millions of dollars gearing up to offer cryptocurrency to their clients. It is now not a matter of if, it is a matter of when. Here are just three examples of positive sentiment towards cryptocurrency from these giant financial firms.

Global investment management fund Blackrock Capital, whose assets are in the trillions of dollars, is headed up by Larry Fink - who is very bullish on cryptocurrencies. Fink has gone on record as saying *"I'm a big believer in the potential of what a cryptocurrency can do."* Chief Investment Strategist Richard Turnill also stated *"We see cryptocurrencies potentially becoming more widely used in the future as the market matures."*

Wellington Capital Management, another trillion dollar firm is sizing up cryptocurrencies. In a report to investors in February, the firm stated they were looking at companies connected to cryptocurrency. The report then went on to say *"Various Wellington teams are already positioning portfolios to take advantage of mining and blockchain implementations by, for example, investing in select chipmakers making components."* So it's not just talk anymore, money is beginning to come in.

Goldman Sachs owned Circle Internet Financial Ltd bought Poloniex, one of the largest cryptocurrency exchanges in the world, for over $400 million. A 9 figure buyout, from a company owned by an investment bank, is a surefire sign that institutional scale money is coming in.

What will government regulation mean for the cryptocurrency space? Is it a good or a bad thing?

The key thing to note is that at the federal level at least - cryptocurrency is not disliked.

Governments want to regulate crypto, to some degree, so they can monitor fraud, and they will take the necessary steps to do this. Now, whether these steps conflict with your moral views towards decentralization is one thing, but regulation is a positive price in terms of price action. Institutional money will only come in if the regulation question is sorted, that is certain.

What is your personal portfolio?

While I won't disclose my exact portfolio of holdings, I will say that it consists of roughly 75% BTC and Ethereum and then the other 25% is split between smaller cap coins. I utilize dollar cost averaging while investing to minimize volatility.

Who are these "whales" people keep talking about?

Good question, simply put, a whale is an individual with high net worth. In the cryptocurrency space, their net worth is measured in cryptocurrency rather than fiat. For example, the top 300 Bitcoin addresses control roughly 25% of the total Bitcoin in circulation.

If you trade regularly you can spot whales by their ability to manipulate the price of coins for their own benefit. They can do this by putting up large buy and sell walls, and also providing huge surges in trading volumes. You must watch out for this if you plan on trading coins with low volume anyway, as these are more easily manipulated. The first major "whale incident" for crypto trading occurred in 2014 when one user sold 30,000 Bitcoin for a price of $300 each. Fortunately, the market was able to recover quickly.

Will there be a crypto ETF within the next 12 months?

This is a big one, both institutional and consumer investors would love to see a cryptocurrency ETF available. The SEC has already rejected 2 Bitcoin ETFs in 2017 due to the volatility issue and the issue of custody. The latter is a case of an independent third party being able to secure the coins within these ETFs so that money managers cannot make off with investor funds. This happens with all other ETFs, but as cryptocurrency doesn't work in the same way as regular ETFs, we are still trying to find a solution that makes all parties happy.

However, as further regulation occurs, and the custody issue is sorted, we will no doubt see more warming towards both a cryptocurrency ETF and a Bitcoin ETF. Whether that will happen in 2018 is uncertain, but I would predict that we will see both of these ETFs within the next 24 months. Obviously one or both of these would be huge for the market.

What is the US stock market's effect on the cryptocurrency market and vice versa?

Thanks to email subscriber Angel D for this one. Now, this is a topic I've looked into very closely over the years, and I can say with a certain degree of certainty that there is zero correlation between the two. In fact, many investors are now looking at the crypto market as a hedge against the stock market.

What do think of owning masternodes as a way of earning passive income?

Thanks to email subscriber Eugene H for this one. This was actually a multi-part question but I condensed the answer into one.

Owning a masternode essentially means you host a certain coin's blockchain on your personal machine. This means you help support the running of the network. This method is an alternative to mining coins.

The majority of masternodes have a minimum amount of coins you must own in order to run one. This is to ensure that the node owner has a significant financial stake in the system, and thus, has less of an incentive to conduct nefarious activity on the network itself.

The big incentive for owning a masternode is that you are rewarded in the form of dividends, these range between 3 and 10% depending on coin. Dash for example offers 7.54% return. PIVX is another decent masternode coin with a 5.74% return, with Navcoin having one with 5% dividends. Be wary of any coins offering ridiculous ROI (at the time of writing, I see one coin offering a 778% annual ROI), these are bonafide scams.

However, the big limiting factor with masternodes is that many of them are just way too expensive for the regular investor. DASH masternodes are around $400,000 a WaltonChain one would be around $130,000 and VeChain around $35,000.

Obsidian represents a good median investment level opportunity for masternode as the 10,000 ODN required would only set you back around $1,400 at the time of writing - with 10% returns. However, you are also taking a risk on a low market cap coin - so you returns could be theoretically worthless.

ROI is obviously important, but there are other factors you should take into account before investing in a masternode for a certain coin. One issue is what percentage of masternodes are owned by a few owners. If only a few parties own the majority of the nodes, they could theoretically band together to attack a coin if they chose to. The other factor is how stable the overall coin value is. Say if you buy a masternode for $10,000 and then the coin's value drops by 50% in the next 3 months, you returns from hosting the node have been drastically reduced. That is why I would only invest in a masternode for a coin you are have already been invested in for a significant period of time.

As a decent middle ground, or if you want to earn passive income without a huge invesment, I like Neo's model of paying out Gas to Neo holders.

How do you choose the coin you invest in?

Thanks to email subscriber Claudio S for this one. Unfortunately, the answer is very boring. It involves painstaking research - Namely the coin whitepaper, YouTube videos by other crypto commentators, checking out GitHub pages and LinkedIn pages for developers.

After that, if I'm still confident (I'd say for every pick there are 5 coins that don't make the cut) then I move forward.

Which coins should I buy if I'm just getting started?

Thanks to email subscriber Jerri C for this one. If you have less than $500, I wouldn't recommend spreading yourself too thin and only starting with one or two coins. You can't go wrong with Bitcoin or Ethereum for these purposes.

If you did want to look at smaller projects, I like Binance Coin (BNB), Ambrosus (AMB) and Jibrel Network (JNT) right now.

ICOs

Are ICOs dead in 2018?

2017 was undoubtedly the year of the ICO. There were 435 successful ICOs with a grand total of over $5.6 billion raised by ICOs throughout the year.

However, they were fraught with talks of scams, development teams running off with the money, and poor execution. As well as projects that didn't really utilize blockchain technology using an ICO as a way to get around SEC regulations for IPOs and raise capital quickly.

The latter point is the most concerning going forward. If cryptocurrency is to progress then we absolutely must stop ICOs being used as a substitute for Kickstarter and Crowdfunding campaigns.

Cryptocurrency at its core is trustless, transparent and decentralized, and many of these ICOs go against one or more of these principles. On top of this, we have seen far too many new investors straight up gambling by throwing their money at these projects with the hope of a quick 10X return.

What we should see is the overall number of projects reduced, but the quality of them rise. This means more projects with a working product, even if its just an MVP, as opposed to a website and a poorly written whitepaper. I'm also intrigued to see how ICOs on Neo and Stellar perform compared to the Ethereum ICOs we saw so many of in 2017. Hopefully, these projects will be able to attract new money into the market while using said money to properly advance their project and give rewards for said investors. We need ICOs to be a viable option if the market is to grow as a whole, due to mass scale cryptocurrency mining being an environmental and logistical problem. ICOs also offer startups a useful way of raising capital while also building a user base at the same time, which the current venture capital model does not.

We may also need additional regulation to prevent poor quality ICOs from being able to get off the ground. Regulation and cryptocurrency are two words that have often been disassociated with one another, but I don't believe regulation would be bad if it weeds out the scammers and only allows legitimate projects to raise funds.

There's also the issue of geographical regulations, for example, China banned its citizens from participating in ICOs in Mid 2017, a move that shocked the market and caused a big dip. If certain projects cannot receive investment from certain countries, then this hampers the goal of payments being truly borderless and again goes against the very essence of cryptocurrency.

So no, I don't believe we will see any "death" of ICOs in 2018 any more than we will see a "death" of cryptocurrency as a whole. The entire ICO craze does need to be cleaned up, and hopefully the market will be able to do some of this "weeding out" process itself as investors become more sophisticated and selective with the projects they choose to invest in, rather than blindly throwing their money at the next flashy ERC20 token.

Why do so many ICOs fail?

Good question, and one that isn't exclusive to cryptocurrencies alone. The vast majority of new startups, blockchain or otherwise, will fail within the first 3 years.

Last year we saw a huge boom in ICOs, with 435 different ones being run, and I would estimate that at least 80% of these will fail in the long term. ICOs garnered tremendous popularity last year, and many of them had no business being in the cryptocurrency space at all. Due to this, we saw a record number of poor quality ICOs. Many of these were never going to be able to execute their projects, and thus, have quickly fallen by the wayside.

In 2018, I predict the overall quality will improve, and we will see more longevity from this next batch of ICOs than we do from many of the 2017 ones.

What are some red flags to look out for before investing in an ICO?

This is an area I've touched on in previous books but it's a vital topic and one which you must be aware of if you don't want to invest in poor quality ICOs.

The biggest red flag is also the one that most people overlook, and that's the whitepaper. You should always read a coin's whitepaper before investing in an ICO. This is the document which lays out, in full, how the coin will work, and how exactly the token itself will be used.

Whitepaper red flags include: Poorly translated whitepapers, plagiarized parts, incomplete white papers which don't offer an explanation on topics. The biggest one of all being no whitepaper available. I would **never** invest an ICO which didn't have a whitepaper available.

The second is the team behind the project. What is their track record? What background do they have with blockchain projects? What background do they have within the industry they aim to disrupt? All these are vital questions that we have to look at. We've even seen cases where poor quality ICOs are using pictures of celebrities as their team members online avatar (see below). Unfortunately, this project still managed to raise over $800,000 before performing an exit scam.

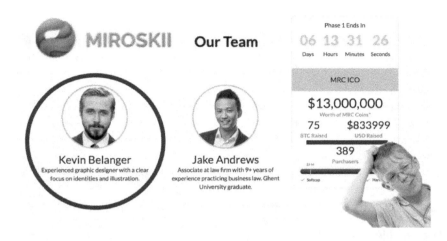

I've previously suggested we will see a decrease in the number of ICOs this year but that we will see an increase in the overall quality of them.

Altcoins

What is Ripple?

Ripple focuses on lowering payment costs in the banking sector via the use of the Ripple network. Designed primarily for financial institutions like banks, Ripple is often referred to as "the banker's coin". Using Ripple makes cross-border payments cheaper than traditional methods like SWIFT. Utilizing lightning fast technology, Ripple can process payments in approximately 4 seconds. The currency was the biggest gainer in 2017 where the coin saw a rise of over 34000%.

Many cryptocurrency purists have been against Ripple day 1 due to its connection with big banks and its centralized nature. The other main criticism lobbied against it was that it is not necessary to use the XRP token to use the Ripple network and thus the token is inherently worthless.

However, Ripple is the coin with the most partnerships with big financial institutions right now, and thus has first mover advantage when it comes to full scale adoption. There are also ongoing rumors that it will be the next coin to be added to Coinbase, which could well result in a huge rush of money coming in because as discussed before, investors see a price of $0.61 and believe it has unlimited room to grow, despite its already large market cap.

Is Steemit/Steem a pyramid scheme?

Now this is an interesting one, for those of you who aren't aware, the Steem itself is based on the social media platform Steemit. Users can publish content such as blog posts and long form articles, and this content is rewarded in the form of digital currency. Similar to how Reddit users receive upvotes, Steemit users receive Steem tokens known as Steem Dollars. The theory behind this being that the financial incentive ensures that users strive to produce quality content.

The elephant in the room is that the Steem founders currently own 80% of the tokens. There has been a lot of rumbling that the large sell orders on Poloniex for Steem tokens are coming from the founders themselves. They also have much higher voting power on the platform than any other user, so in theory, could just transfer huge amounts to their friends by upvoting certain posts. One of the biggest criticisms lobbied at the platform is that all the highest upvoted posts (the ones receiving the most money), are pro Steemit posts. This combined with the ability to instantly cash out your Steem already leads to way too much selling pressure.

Which leads us to a followup question of "how can it be workable long term?"

They will have to continue to "print" more Steem to pay for new content, that much is certain. The initial supply inflation was 100% per year, for comparison Bitcoin's was 100% for the first year and is currently projected to be 5% for this year. New users are suffering because their posts are simply not gaining enough traction for them to build a following, which is an issue we have seen with multiple social networks including YouTube and Instagram. Then there is the issue of bot accounts upvoting content from fellow bot accounts which can be boiled down to rich making each other richer. So I can see the argument for a "pyramid" like dependency where new users have to come in Steem to be worth anything, and if new users don't think it's worth it to post content anymore - then we could indeed see a sharp drop in Steem's value.

Essentially, the biggest problem for the platform right now is the conflict between the promotional material pertaining to "being paid to post" and the actual distribution of rewards on the site. Too much voting power is in the hands of too few users right now, and this can influence price in a number of ways.

That being said, I don't believe the project is a "pyramid scheme" in the traditional nefarious sense of the word. Their token economics may not be the best, and the concentration of wealth is concerning. But this can be fixed with a rework in their reward algorithm. The team have accomplished a lot, and their large user base should be admired. But the long term potential for the project is not without scrutiny, and without fixing some element of the reward system, I can't see how the project will pan out 5 or 10 years down the line.

Where is best place to buy altcoins like Ripple, Stellar and Neo?

If you've been in this space for a while, you'll now understand that there are many more investment options than just the 4 coins on Coinbase.

The most popular of these is Ripple, with Stellar and Neo being two more large projects within the top 10 that have received a lot of publicity in past 6 months. However, it is hard for investors to buy these for fiat currency, so we must buy them using cryptocurrency like Bitcoin, Ethereum or Litecoin.

I personally recommend <u>Binance</u> (use the QR code if you are reading the paperback edition of this book) if you are looking to buy, sell or trade any altcoins. They have by far and away the best customer support of any cryptocurrency exchange. In addition to allowing Ethereum trading pairs for all coins. There are currently over 100 coins you can trade on Binance and they have very competitive trading fees of just 0.1%

I should note I no longer recommend Bittrex as they have stopped allowing registrations from US customers. Other exchanges I have personally used to buy smaller altcoins are Liqui and Cryptopia.

Is Dogecoin a joke or a real cryptocurrency?

One of the oldest coins around, Dogecoin started as a fun project and ended up with actual monetary value. Because of the coin's ability to facilitate micropayments (usually a few cents) - Dogecoin's value largely comes from an internet form of "tipping". The most prominent example of this is holders donating Dogecoin to Reddit users for posts they enjoyed reading.

The coin was never meant to be a long term investment, or be a trading tool against other currencies. The community's price slogan of "1 doge = 1 doge" is an indicator of this. So unless you're planning on using it for tipping or just as a fun introduction to cryptocurrencies, I wouldn't buy a ton of Doge expecting it to rise anytime soon.

If I buy XRP, am I investing in cryptocurrency or Ripple Labs?

Thanks to email subscriber Roberta K for this one. There is a big distinction to be made here, if you buy XRP tokens on Binance or wherever, you **are not** buying shares of Ripple Labs. They operate as a separate entity, and XRP tokens are merely the native token of the Ripple protocol. XRP is what is destroyed to cover transaction fees of banks using the Ripple network.

So the value of XRP is indeed linked to the success of the Ripple payment network, but it is not a linear ratio. The Ripple network has the ability to operate without XRP if necessary.

Which coin has the fastest transaction time?

Speed is one of the most imperative factors in examining a coin, especially the ones aiming to be payment facilitators. For example, Bitcoin transactions take an average of 10 minutes to complete, and the network itself can process roughly 7 transactions per second. Ethereum's network is sightly faster at roughly 20 transactions per second.

The Visa network on the other hand processes roughly 7000 transactions per second. Ripple is the current leader in the crypto world for this and processes roughly 1,500 transactions per second on its network - which makes it roughly 10 times faster than PayPal for example. Other coins like Stellar Lumens and Nano pride themselves on fast transaction times but don't have the volume of the Ripple network to put these to the test.

Then there are a number of other projects that claim to be able to process transactions faster. XtraBytes (XBY) for example has patent pending technology that the team claim could process "up to 100,000 transactions per second". Other coins like RChain claim speeds of 40,000 transactions per second. Though I should note these are purely theoretical or have only been achieved in a pure low volume test environment - thus have not been "battle tested" so to speak.

Do you believe in technicals or fundamentals when analyzing a project?

Thanks to email subscriber Munish M for this one. I am a long term value investor first and foremost. I would rather invest in a great project at an OK price than try to make a quick buck because of some short term price action on a project I feel is just ''OK''. This market is so volatile that I believe in the best projects, even if they have 50% dips, we've seen it for so many of the good projects, and they always come back stronger.

Is Electroneum (ETN) a scam?

Another scam question, these appear to be very popular. Electroneum boasts about being the first British cryptocurrency. The ICO raised the expected hard cap amount well before the deadline. However, since then, the project has been hit by a number of developments which are a cause for concern for those who participated in the ICO.

Part of the hype surrounding the project was that mobile mining was possible, with numbers of 70ETN per day using a Samsung Galaxy S8 claimed. Many users are reporting rewards closer to 1ETN per day. Obviously, some room for error is expected, but for that estimate to be wrong by that amount is concerning. Either the development team exaggerated the potential reward pool, or the technology is not working as they would have hoped. There was also a security breach in November that had a number of users concerned about the team's technical ability to deal with situations like this. Lack of exchange listings have also been cause for concern, as a listing on Kucoin continues to be delayed for unspecified reasons. Perhaps the most concerning of all is that updates from the team themselves have been getting *less* frequent in recent months.

That being said, I haven't seen any nefarious acts from the team themselves and I doubt outright scam would be the right word to use, it seems to me that the project is just going through growing pains right now. Mobile mining is a fairly novel concept and one that remains to be seen whether it is viable in the long term. I'd still say the project is one to keep tabs on, but one you should monitor closely if you are already holding ETN.

Is Monero (XMR) really just for drug dealers and criminals?

One of the biggest gainers of 2016, and currently the number 11 coin by market capitalization, Monero has gotten a bad reputation over the past year due to its complete anonymity for those using it. Bitcoin, on the other hand, is "pseudo-anonymous" in the sense that you could trace transactions back to a person if you can identify one of their transactions. Monero came to mainstream attention in 2016 after it was revealed to be the currency of choice for users of AlphaBay, an underground drug dealing website. Monero proved itself to be truly private after law enforcement officials simply could not work out just how much XMR the AlphaBay owner had in his possession.

The thing is though, you don't need to be a criminal kingpin or even a small time drug dealer to have the need, or want, for privacy. The biggest one of these being that privacy makes you less vulnerable to cyber attacks. For example, we know exactly how much Bitcoin the largest wallets in the world hold, and the identities of some of these wallet owners are known, which in turn makes them a target for thieves. Monero on the other hand makes this impossible, and thus, keeps the owners safety as a priority.

This isn't the first time the crypto space has had accusation like this levied at it. Bitcoin was previously under scrutiny during the days of underground drug market Silk Road. However, it has seen cleaned up its act and it is now estimated that less than 1% of Bitcoin transactions are for illegal goods or money laundering. There are also a number of other coin which claim to be anonymous but don't quite deliver on this promise on the same level as Monero - namely ZCash and Dash.

What kind of asset do the US government consider cryptocurrency?

Now, this is a confusing one as it has certain tax implications. So cryptocurrencies are *not* considered securities like regular stocks. Nor are they consider to be commodities like gold and silver. They are actually considered to be property of all things. That means they are still under the same short and long term capital gains but do not fall under wash sale rules like regular stocks. You can however still write off losses.

Which cryptocurrency projects have working products right now?

I took this to mean projects that are out of the alpha and beta stages and have full use of their platform online available for the public (or their industry) to use.

We'll start with the coins that are fully functioning. We have the coins which are purely payment orientated like Bitcoin, Monero, Ripple, Dash. These are work as intended as peer to peer transaction systems. Then we have to include the big smart contracts platforms like Ethereum and NEM. As well as the coins which are linked to exchanges like Binance Coin and KuCoin Shares. Now we have these out of the way, we can look at some more interesting uses of blockchain technology, we are already implemented.

Navcoin's mobile wallet is now out of the beta stages and allows currency transfers with optional private payments.

Basic Attention Token has their brave browser up and running, although it remains to be seen what kind of long term adoption they will get when competing against Chrome and Safari.

DENT (not to be confused with Dentacoin) have a working mobile app which allows users to top-up and earn free mobile data. Currently, it works in the US and Mexican markets but more countries are planned for later this year.

WABI has RFID and counterfeit protection rolled out in multiple department stores, with over 1000 stores planned across China by the end of the year.

Bounty0x, kind of blockchain version of Fiverr/Upwork/Mechanical Turk which offers crypto rewards in return for doing small tasks, is already up and running with 381 jobs currently online.

Will Ethereum overtake Bitcoin this year?

This is probably the most popular question I've seen in the past 3 months. Will "the flippening" as many call it, happen in 2018? For this to occur, we'd need to see Ethereum's price go to roughly 20% of Bitcoin's, and thus, due to Ethereum's larger supply, the overall market cap would be bigger. At the time of writing, if Bitcoin stays at around $8,500, we'd need to see Ethereum at $1,600 for this to happen.

Now the closest we've come to this before is seeing Ethereum/Bitcoin ratio at around 0.12 in June last year. That was before the late 2017 bull run where Bitcoin once again took off and ran away from the pack so to speak.

For Ethereum to overtake Bitcoin in the next 12 months, we'd need both overwhelmingly positive news for Ethereum, in turn with some negative sentiment towards Bitcoin. The former could be achieved with implemented the Casper protocol which would see Ethereum move over from a Proof of Work model to a Proof of Stake one, however, this looks increasingly unlikely to happen before 2019 now.

We would also need to see success from more of the ERC20 tokens. If you're not aware, 80 of the top 100 cryptocurrency projects right now are running on the Ethereum network, which is a big part of what makes Ethereum so successful. Many of these projects are still in the early stages of development, so if we can see the teams hit their roadmap targets, and receive more attention, then this will, in turn, lead to positive move going forward.

The third factor is that of trading pairs. Will more traders switch from Bitcoin pairings to Ethereum pairings for buying altcoins? If you're new to the market, you might not be aware that until 2017, it was pretty much impossible to buy altcoins with anything other than Bitcoin as a trading pair. Now, the major altcoin exchanges all feature Ethereum pairings for the vast majority of the coins they offer. Binance, for example, now has ETH/ALT pairings for 101 out of the 104 coins it offers. That being said, traders still seem to favor Bitcoin pairings, mainly because the ones doing the large trades have accumulated a large amount of Bitcoin, and thus that is the coin they have the necessary liquidity in to perform such big trades. If we start seeing more volume for Ethereum pairings then will lead to a push in the price of Ethereum.

The second part of this whole equation is that we would probably need some negative Bitcoin news. However, this then poses another problem in that whenever Bitcoin's price drops significantly, it pulls the rest of the market down with it, including Ethereum. The theory behind this is that when we have bad news regarding Bitcoin, people convert their Bitcoin back to fiat rather than putting it in altcoins. This is also the reason we see altcoins go down when Bitcoin goes on a run because new money entering the market only goes into Bitcoin. Historically, altcoins have performed best with Bitcoin's price has been stagnant for a while, as this is when new investors move their money from Bitcoin into other crypto ventures.

So you can see it's not quite as simple as just waiting for Ethereum to overtake Bitcoin, a number of stars would have to align so to speak. I still think it's entirely possible in the long run that Ethereum could be the number one cryptocurrency, but I don't see it happening in 2018.

Could Litecoin be worth more than Bitcoin Cash?

This is another, could coin X be worth more than coin Y question which I received via email. Looking at market capitalization at the time of writing. We have Litecoin worth roughly 60% of Bitcoin Cash in terms of market cap.

Both of these coins have hurdles to overcome going forward. Litecoin, which positions itself as a cheaper, faster Bitcoin, has growing competition from other coins which focus on the microtransactions space, with Nano being the biggest threat right now. Litecoin does have first mover advantage, and if their payment processor Litepay is adopted by a lot of companies, then we could see a push for Litecoin. Litecoin also has the advantage of "being the cheapest coin on Coinbase" and as such, receives a lot of new money that comes into the market during bullish periods.

Bitcoin Cash, on the other hand, has a more questionable future ahead. It saw a run at the end of last year, in what was one of the most exciting days in 2017 where the price soared from $800 to over $2100 dollars in a day and reach the #2 spot in terms of market capitalization. However, recently, Bitcoin transactions have actually been faster *and* cheaper than Bitcoin Cash transactions, which was the latter's big selling point. It was added to Coinbase in January 2018, but without the network effects that Bitcoin has, I really can't see a clear path for Bitcoin Cash going forward unless the team undergoes a full rebrand, which could even end up hurting it even more.

Long term, I am more bullish on Litecoin as a potential project, so I can certainly see the market cap being worth more than Bitcoin Cash.

Why are there so many supply chain tokens?

This could be rephrased as "why are there so many cryptocurrency tokens" - but we'll focus on the supply chain side of things.

Supply chain management is one of the initial areas in which blockchain has a real world use case. Whether it is medicine, food or other consumer goods, blockchain technology can help prevent fraud, counterfeit goods while ensuring safe transportation from one party to another. For manufacturers, it combines with the Internet of Things economy and helps monitor various transport conditions to ensure the product is delivered both on time, and in the required condition.

Blockchain's publicly verifiable ledger means that anyone can see that there has not been any tampering with a product during the transportation stage. In other words, they can see that the carton of milk they are buying really is milk. This might not seem to be a big issue for those of you in the West. But in China, counterfeit food is a real problem. We've seen baby formulas laced with Melamine, lamb which was actually rat meat and a statistic that up to 70% of the wine in the country is falsely labeled. Needless to say, in China at least, fake food has now become an epidemic.

Hence why we have so many coins focusing on the supply chain sector. We have Modum out of Switzerland, which monitors medical goods. We also have Chinese products like WaltonChain, which focuses on RFID technology, as well as, Wabi and VeChain. And also smaller ones like Ambrosus. These projects are also competing with traditional companies developing their own blockchain solutions for supply chain management.

The important thing to remember is, there won't be one "winner" when it comes to these tokens, the supply chain sector is so broad that many different tokens can peacefully co-exist without eating into each other's market share.

Unlike pure payment coins, which usually compete directly against each other, we could also see a number of these supply chain tokens collaborate with one another, to share technology, and help develop a better solution for consumers and manufacturers alike.

What's the difference between Bitcoin and Bitcoin Cash?

So by now, we're all familiar with Bitcoin, but some of you may be wondering exactly what Bitcoin Cash is, and its role in the cryptocurrency economy.

Bitcoin Cash (BCH) emerged as the result of a split or "hard fork" in the Bitcoin technology on August 1st 2017. The end-goal of Bitcoin Cash is to function as a global currency, in the founder's words, to be what Bitcoin was supposed to have been in line with the original vision for Bitcoin outlined in the 2008 whitepaper.

The split occurred out of problems with Bitcoin's ability to process transactions at a high speed. As the network continues to grow, so do waiting times for transactions. BCC aims to run more transactions, as well as, providing lower transactions fees. One of the major solutions to this issue is increasing the size of each block so that more data can be processed at once. Bitcoin Cash increases the block size to 8MB, as opposed to the 1MB size of Bitcoin.

However, as of the time of writing, Bitcoin actually had lower transaction fees than Bitcoin Cash, so it seems like the change hasn't really worked. You also have to consider Bitcoin's network effect, in other words, how many people are aware of it and use it on a regular basis - which is obviously much more in favor of Bitcoin than Bitcoin Cash.

Listing on Coinbase did help Bitcoin Cash in the short term, but it remains to be seen if the two coin can co-exist in the long run. If I was a betting man, and I had to put all my money on one coin surviving, I'd choose Bitcoin.

What do you think of APPICS (XAP)

Thanks to email subscriber Mike D for this one. APPICS is the first ICO built on top of the STEEM platform, and operates in the same vein. It is a social media platform that rewards participation with cryptocurrency. However, APPICS sees itself as more of a competitor to Instagram as it will focus on the mobile space and the sharing of pictures and videos.

The main concern is that it will use the same token economics as STEEM, which is that "power users" are given a large number of XAP tokens and thus have large voting power. I previously expressed my dislike of this model in discussing the STEEM platform itself, and the same potential for manipulation occurs in the APPICS model as well. APPICS furthers my concern with their use of "judges" for each category. A pre-selected social media influencer or influencers will have a large holding of XAP tokens and can use these to select content they believe is worthy of big rewards. This is anything but a decentralized model and could almost be called blockchain nepotism.

APPICS also promises to integrate point of sale shopping for its tokens, in other words, you can directly spend tokens in stores which accept them.

At the time of writing, the coin is currently in the final stages of its ICO which the aim of raising around $18 million. The website doesn't have much information beyond what I've written here, with a basic whitepaper and a limited FAQ section.

Overall, it's a good concept, but there is a lot of competition in the incentivized blockchain social media space. I can see the idea being attractive to content creators, but just how much they will be able to encourage user adoption of the platform I'm not sure.

Miscellaneous Questions

Could the Rothchilds bring down cryptocurrency?

Thanks to email subscriber Mark M for this one. The Rothchild's, and other world's financial elite do not have a hold on cryptocurrency as they do not control a large portion of any of the funds.

It's plausible that they could manipulate a smaller token for their own gain. Others have rumored that as Ripple focuses on the banking sector, the financial elite owns large portions of this. However, these are just rumors and I wouldn't hold put too much thought into them.

Will blockchain technology cause people to lose jobs?

Blockchain technology is game changing in the level of trustless automation it will provide. The negative side of this is that it could well impact the job security of those working in certain industries.

The biggest ones in the early stages will be low level financial positions such as bookkeepers and mortgage lenders. Blockchain could easily streamline these processes and eliminate the need for a human being. There are also impacts for those in the banking and security industries for the same reason. Supply chain management is another area in which blockchain technology has the potential to greatly impact.

Now, I wouldn't go as far as some commentators who cry that "all accountants will be made obsolete within 10 years", but there will definitely be a downsizing in certain industries.

How do you spot a cryptocurrency scam?

Like any space that has money flowing into it, there are a number of bad actors and people with nefarious intentions. Cryptocurrency is no different in this respect. In the past 6 months, there have been a number of high profile scams. The most notable of which was Bitconnect - a cryptocurrency lending platform.

Bitconnect claimed they had a cryptocurrency trading bot which made investors guaranteed returns of 40% *per month*. Now, we must remember that Bernie Madoff, who ran the largest pyramid scheme in Wall Street history, was only delivering investors 8-12% *per year.* Any project with promises of "guaranteed returns" should be avoided.

How the scam worked was the same way all pyramid schemes worked. It funneled money from new investors into the pockets of older investors. And when the money stopped coming in, the project collapsed upon itself. In December, Bitconnect received cease and desist letters from various authorities and then pulled an exit scam causing the price to drop roughly 95% in just a few days.

There have been a few "successors" to Bitconnect in the form of Davorcoin and Falcon coin. Both of which have the same model of promising investors guaranteed returns. Fortunately, both of these have since shut down and had less of a lifespan than Bitconnect. There will doubtless be another pyramid or Ponzi scheme that pops up like this in the near future, so stay well away from any project that promises guaranteed returns.

Why does Warren Buffett keep badmouthing cryptocurrency?

There are a few Warren Buffett quotes floating around regarding Bitcoin and cryptocurrency as a whole. Including ones such as *"I can say with almost certainty that they will come to a bad ending."* as well as calling Bitcoin *"a mirage"*.

What we need to remember is that Buffett earned his wealth from investing in fundamentals, and in his own words "only investing things I understand". In the same interview with the first quote above, he finished with *"I get into enough trouble with the things I think I know something about. Why in the world should I take a long or short position in something I don't know about?"*.

Over the years, Buffett has been famously reluctant to touch new technology as an investment, preferring more to focus on companies with a long standing history. His self-admitted previous "misses" so to speak include Amazon, Apple and Google. The latter of which he apologized to investors, for not recognizing the potential of Google, at a Berkshire Hathaway annual meeting in 2017.

So it's not that Buffett is so bearish on cryptocurrencies and blockchain technology as a whole, he just doesn't understand them, and thus investing in them would go against his entire investment philosophy.

Why do so many cryptocurrencies rebrand?

That's a very good question, in the past year we've seen two high profile coins rebrand. First, we had Antshares rebrand as Neo, then we had RaiBlocks rebrand as Nano.

One of the big reasons behind this is that many projects see rebranding as an opportunity for increased adoption of their platform. For example <Word>Chain is seen by some analysts as juvenile and amateurish, while others see it as limiting investment to within the cryptocurrency space.

There's also the case of logo rebrands. In the Antshares example, the logo changed from a cartoon ant which could have been drawn by a 13 year old, to a more slick green logo. Nano's logo change also used the name to represent the unique block lattice design of the network, whereas the previous RaiBlocks logo could have been a default Symbol in MS Paint.

Other see rebranding as merely a chance for a coin to get its name into the media again. Especially during a down period in the development cycle. Both Nano and Neo received large bumps in price after rebranding so there could be some credence to this theory.

Is mining cryptocurrencies profitable for the average person?

The answer to this is simple. In 99.9% of cases, if you live in a country where you *do not* have access to dirt cheap electricity, then mining cryptocurrency will be a net negative. That is without considering the large investment you require up front to get your hands on the latest mining equipment like top of the line ASIC rigs. The most successful mining operations are all ones that have invested a minimum of 7 figures up front, and often this figure is in the tens of millions of dollars.

You are much better off buying and holding coins if you are a beginner. If you have financial trading experience than trading can also be profitable.

Are people *really* getting rich with cryptocurrency?

Yes, without a shadow of a doubt, more regular folks have gotten rich with cryptocurrency than with any other financial instrument in the past 20 years. We are currently witnessing the birth of a new asset class not seen since the days of the DOTCOM boom.

How long is "long term" in cryptocurrency?

Cryptocurrency isn't like a stock where we'd consider long term to be 10+ years. The stock market moves much slower, and the cycles themselves move extremely quickly. The majority of this is because cryptocurrency has always been around in the internet age. The age of interconnectivity where everything can be done at the touch of a button. Whereas stocks and bonds were formed at an age of having to call brokers. There's also the wild card of having a 24/7 365 market in cryptocurrency, something that no other financial asset possesses.

When the Nasdaq crashed in 2003 after the dotcom boom, it took almost 15 years for it to return to the highs seen in the year 2000. Conversely, when Bitcoin had its first big "crash" in 2013, it returned to new highs within just 2 years. So needless to say, the crypto market moves *a lot* faster than traditional financial markets.

Therefore when we're talking long term with cryptocurrency, we're often talking about periods of no more than 18-24 months. This applies to both price cycles and development roadmaps for newer cryptocurrency projects.

What are the best YouTube channels?

The following YouTube channels are ones I personally subscribe to and feature solid, unbiased cryptocurrency information, and more importantly **do not promote** any scam cryptocurrency schemes or projects. I should note that I am not affiliated with any of these channels in any way.

Boxmining - Michael provides daily cryptocurrency market analysis, and his ability to speak Chinese gives him unprecedented access to interesting Chinese cryptocurrency projects such as WaltonChain.

Crypto Bobby - Has a bunch of interviews with figures behind major cryptocurrency projects.

Coin Mastery - Objective analysis of many different cryptocurrency projects without the hype

Doug Polk - Doug has taken it upon himself to call out scammers in the cryptocurrency space, doing us all a public service in the process.

Ameer Rosic - The founder of BlockGeeks, an online cryptocurrency education platform, he focuses more on the big picture and blockchain technology as a whole. His videos tend to be on the longer side and provide a more in-depth analysis.

Coin Bloq - This is a new one that I've just started following, they do in depth, level headed reviews of some more obscure ICOs and altcoins.

Where are the best places to store my coins?

There are 3 options to store your coins. You can keep them online on an exchange, which I only recommend if you are holding small amounts. The important thing to note with exchanges is that you do not hold your private key, the exchange does. This is still the case if you use the Coinbase Vault as opposed to the regular Coinbase wallet.

Your private key is what you need to spend your coins and transfer them out of your wallet. Therefore if the exchange gets hacked, your private key can be stolen by hackers.

The other options, in which you do hold your private key, are to take your coins "offline" in either a paper or a hardware wallet. Both of these represent a more secure long-term storage solution.

Paper Wallets:

Paper wallets are simply notes of your private key that are written down on paper. They will often feature QR codes so the sender can quickly scan them to send cryptocurrency.

Pros:

- Cheap - your only cost is the paper you print them on

- Relatively simple to set up

- Your private keys are not stored digitally, and are therefore not subject to cyber-attacks or hardware failures.

Cons:

- Loss of paper due to human error

- Paper is fragile and can degrade quickly in certain environments

- Not easy to spend cryptocurrency quickly if necessary - not useful for everyday transactions

Recommendations:

It is recommended you store your paper wallet in a sealed plastic bag to protect against water or damp conditions. If you are holding cryptocurrency for the long-term, store the paper inside a safe.

Ensure you read and understand the step-by-step instructions before printing any paper wallets.

Bitcoin:

http://bitaddress.org

http://bitcoinpaperwallet.com

Ethereum:

http://myetherwallet.com/

Litecoin:

https://liteaddress.org/

Hardware wallets:

The Ledger Nano S is still the best of the hardware wallets on the market. Plus, they are finally back in stock after a 3 month drought on the official website. Note, only buy your Ledger Nano from the official site (http://ledgerwallet.com) as a number of counterfeit models which steal your private keys have popped up on third party websites.

What are the biggest problems facing businesses who want to accept cryptocurrency?

I found this one on Reddit and thought it'd make a good discussion topic. Many business owners are now seeing adoption for crypto increase, and examining how accepting it as a payment method could benefit their business.

The big issue right now though is volatility, no one wants to accept something that could lose 50% of its value in less than a month. There are workaround solutions to this, for example, BitPay is a point of sale operator which converts cryptocurrency to fiat at the end of every working day. However, BitPay had its own issues with slower transaction times.

Transaction fees are also an issue, which is why coins focusing on micropayments like Nano and Ripple may well have an advantage in this area.

What is the cryptocurrency tax situation?

The cryptocurrency tax situation is a complicated one, and depending on where you live will vary tremendously. The big thing to note is that if you have simply bought and held to this point, you have not incurred any taxable events.

There is also the question of short and long term capital gains tax. In other words, you owe more if you sell an asset within 1 year of buying it than you do for selling it after holding for more than a year.

Conclusion

And there we go, answers to all of your burning cryptocurrency and blockchain questions.

First of all, I'd like to thank everyone who submitted questions via email or on various forums, it was great fun answering them all, and I hope my answers can benefit many more people as a result of this book.

As per usual, I'll finish with my standard recommendations of doing additional research on top of what you read in this book, and never invest more than you can afford to lose.

I wish you the best of luck in the cryptocurrency market, and I hope you make a lot of money.

Thanks,

Stephen

P.S. If you sign up for Coinbase using this link, you will receive $10 worth of free Bitcoin after your first purchase of more than $100 worth of cryptocurrency.

CPSIA information can be obtained
at www.ICGtesting.com
Printed in the USA
BVHW051542160921
616891BV00012BA/984